What to Listen for in Music

BOOKS BY AARON COPLAND

Our New Music

Music and Imagination

What to Listen for in Music

AARON COPLAND

What to Listen for
in Music

with AN INTRODUCTION BY
WILLIAM SCHUMAN

McGraw-Hill Book Company

New York   St. Louis   San Francisco
Hamburg   London   Mexico   Toronto

1 2 3 4 5 6 7 8 9 FGR FGR 8 9 2 1 0 9 8

ISBN 0-07-013091-4

LIBRARY OF CONGRESS CATALOGING-IN-PUBLICATION DATA

Copland, Aaron, 1900–
    What to listen for in music.

    1. Music appreciation.   I. Title.
MT6.C78W4   1989   780'.1'5   87-27569
ISBN 0-07-013091-4

Contents

[v]

Contents

Introduction

F OR the innocent music lover it must seem strange indeed to read a how-to book on the subject of listening to music. Since when are there problems in listening to music? Music is there to be enjoyed. Why should one have to learn or need guidance on how to listen to what one is hearing? And why would one of our great composers take time from composing to write

Introduction

a primer on music? The answer is simple. Listening to music is a skill that is acquired through experience and learning. Knowledge enhances enjoyment.

Musicians are accustomed to the prose of composers as critics and as writers of learned theses on technical subjects (Berlioz, Schoenberg, Strauss and, closer to home, Babbitt, Piston, Persichetti are but a few of the many names that come to mind), but before Copland no master composer had ever attempted to explain the craft of music composition to the layperson. This book is one of a kind, in fact, unique. The uninitiated can gauge its significance by imagining a book by Rembrandt called *What to Look for in Painting*.

To begin to appreciate *What to Listen for in Music* it is well to remind ourselves of just who the author of this book is. The music of Aaron Copland is recognized as part of our heritage. That special Copland sound has enriched us all. It is a sound that was not in music before, and so personal an expression that not one of his many imitators has been able to make it convincingly his own. Yet Aaron Copland has so long been a familiar figure in our national musical life that he and his work are too easily taken for granted. Surely we glory in his achievements and count our good fortune in his presence, but are we sufficiently aware of his singular qualities? What makes Copland so special?

Introduction

Any outstanding creative artist is, to be sure, special, but Copland has created a body of works that speaks to his countrymen in identifiable terms—and this identification is national commonality. By whatever description, Copland's art evokes a response based on our shared experiences, and gives us a sense of belonging. But Copland's *What to Listen for in Music* is yet another example of the broad leadership that Copland has exercised these many years.

A number of his colleagues, myself included, have had many opportunities to speak and write about Aaron Copland. In recalling some previous statements the same observations recur. Foremost for me is my firm conviction that he represents the ideal for artists functioning in a democratic society. Copland's roles are many and varied—citizen, composer, performer, teacher, lecturer, committee member, spokesperson, and lest we forget one of his favorites, conductor. *What to Listen for in Music* represents Copland the professor and gives us an accurate indication of his teaching philosophy.

As teachers of composition, composers more often than not tend to impose their own views on their students and to instill adherence to their own technical procedures. Copland is that rare composer who helps his students find their own means of expressing themselves, rather than mastering his own techniques, which

Introduction

may or may not be germane to their particular talents. Copland combines the scholar's knowledge of music of the past with an encyclopedic understanding of all contemporary music. As an outcome of his extraordinary knowledge and clear philosophy reflected in his approach to teaching, his pupils compose in a variety of styles. A less doctrinaire attitude would be difficult to imagine. In essence, Copland is saying that an effective teacher can have his own strong convictions, yet feel it an obligation to expose his pupils to esthetic doctrines and technical procedures with which he himself may not be in particular sympathy, but which seem right for the pupil. Here is the opposite of the authoritarian—concern for the nature of the individual and not with the imposition of a priori conclusions.

Granted that Copland is the quintessential artist in a democratic society, I have often wished nevertheless that we could bestow a regal title. In England he would long since have been referred to as Sir Aaron and have been designated an official national composer. But titles simply do not go with the charm and directness of the Copland makeup. I can recall over twenty-five years ago referring to him as the Dean of American Composers, and how bemused he was. He continues gallantly to bear this title.

If we lack a duly constituted national entity em-

Introduction

powered to grant honorific titles, we have another mechanism that is even more meaningful: the judgment of one's peers. Copland is preeminent and the object of our affection and esteem. It gives us satisfaction to tell him so. He accepts the accolades of his colleagues and public with unfailing grace and good humor. When I asked him if at long last he wasn't sated with all the honors he said: "Bill, you underestimate my capacity!"

The contents of *What to Listen for in Music* take the reader from the simplest elements of music through the gradual unfolding of its most complex aspects. The book in a way is analogous to the author's music, for Copland's repertory ranges from the most accessible popular works to chamber music of the most distilled and esoteric erudition.

In the popular works, for example, "Appalachian Spring," Copland provides a special musical insight into a sentiment recognizably indigenous. In "A Lincoln Portrait" the musical frame embodies the text and gives an added dimension to Lincoln's compassionate utterances. In these works, and compositions such as "Rodeo" and "Billy the Kid," Copland transforms traditional American folk materials into the most sophisticated art by discerning the potentialities in simple music that could be perceived only by an artist with extraordinary imagination.

To the uninitiated it could almost seem as though

Introduction

the Copland of these popular works and the so-called "serious" Copland were two separate composers at work. Not so, for the same Copland sound that informs the popular music is present also in the more complicated masterworks. He has created in every medium: from songs, chamber music, and chorus to theater, film, opera, and symphony.

With a reminder again that *What to Listen for in Music* has been written by one of the great composers of history, turn now to its pages, knowing you are the privileged student of a master. If you will study the Table of Contents, you will observe the gradual unfolding of a complicated subject in step-by-step fashion. The book is clearly based on the premise that the more you know about the subject of music, the greater will be your joy in listening to it. The first prerequisite for listening to music is so obvious that it almost seems ludicrous to mention, yet it is often the single element that is absent: to pay attention and to give the music your concentrated effort as an active listener.

It is revealing to compare the actions of theater audiences to those of symphonic audiences. In the theater the audience listens with full attention to every line of the play, knowing that if important lines are missed understanding can be diminished—this instinctive attention is too often lacking in the concert hall.

Introduction

One has but to observe listeners at a concert to witness the distractions of talking or reading or simply staring into space. Only a small percentage is vitally concerned with the essential role of active listening. This lack is serious because the listener is essential to the process of music; music after all consists of the composer, the performer, and the listener. Each of these three elements should be present in the most ideal way. We expect a fine composition brilliantly performed, but how often do we think that it should also be brilliantly heard?

The destiny of a piece of music, while basically in the hands of the composer and performer, also depends on the attitude and ability of the listener. It is the listener in the larger sense who dictates the ultimate acceptance or rejection of the composition and performer. Musicians know full well from experience that the same music with the same performers can be received with drastic differences by varying audiences. In other words, the perceived quality of music is clearly at the mercy of the actual quality of its auditors. Unfortunately for music, many listeners are content to sit in an emotional bath and limit their reaction to music to the sensuous element of being surrounded by sounds. But the sounds are organized; the sounds have intellectual as well as emotional appeal.

The adventure of learning how to listen to music is

Introduction

one of the great joys of exposure to this art. Listening is a subject that can be taught and this book organizes and clarifies approaches to this subject. Reading the book unaided will not suddenly make you a virtuoso listener, but it can set you on the path. Your efforts to understand more of what is taking place will be rewarded a thousand-fold in the intense pleasure and increased interest you will find.

There is much music of course that requires no special attention for enjoyment. Music serves a wide gamut of appetites, and comparisons to a well-planned menu illustrate the point. An appetizer, after all, is meant to titillate, a principal course is meant to nourish, and a dessert is meant as a pleasant afterthought to send people on their way. If you examine the programs of symphony orchestras you will find that in general this principle abounds, that is to say, the overture, the symphony, and the contrasting lighter ending. Sometimes the musical meal is all of the main-course variety. Sometimes, as in special "pops" concerts, it is mostly appetizers and desserts. But the point to be made is that the nature of each piece of music defines its purpose, and the realization of the implied purpose indicates the success or failure of the composition, performer, and listener.

Our musical appetizers and desserts do not require

Introduction

the special understanding necessary for listening to music of great weight and complication. This in no way diminishes the worth of "light" music. There is after all no such thing as an unacceptable kind of music—only varying qualitative examples from good to bad within each kind. These distinctions are especially important to emphasize at a time in history when there is so much talk about the equal worth of all kinds of music.

Popular music has a special purpose: to entertain while demanding the least amount of effort on the part of those exposed. To attempt to compare the worth of popular music with that of so-called serious music is a non-issue. Getting back to our food analogy, the prime sources of our nourishment do not invalidate the frills that surround them. To honor all kinds of music without false claims of illogical comparisons is to enjoy as our natures dictate the varying appeals of diverse efforts. We take pleasure and inspiration in reading novels, poetry, and philosophy of the most profound nature, while at the same time derive pleasure in relaxing with an attractive magazine.

The above is not to imply that the musical counterpart of junk food is bad for your health, but rather that a diet restricted to one kind of art is limiting. This book should help listeners who have a curiosity about more

Introduction

complicated forms of music. And make no mistake about it: great music is born of great effort by great and dedicated minds and by greatly devoted listeners. The number of people who listen to music of this character are but an insignificant percentage of those whose waking hours are saturated with sounds as omnipresent as the air we breathe.

Copland's book in the final analysis is a book of propaganda. It is a book written by a man deeply committed to spreading the Gospel of what in less self-conscious days we could refer to as "good music." The book is an invitation, and one that you would do well to accept.

William Schuman
NEW YORK CITY
1988

Author's Note for the 1957 Edition

A LMOST twenty years have passed since the first
edition of this book was issued in 1939. It is
naturally gratifying to me to know that it has continued to be found useful by music listeners since that
time, both in America and abroad.*

During the past two decades we have witnessed
an unprecedented spread of interest in all forms of
music throughout the world. Both the quantity and
quality of music listening has changed, but fortunately for the author, the basic problems of "what to
listen for" have remained about the same. For that reason, only minor corrections were needed in the body
of the text.

Two new chapters have been added—one on the
thorny question of how present-day composition
should be listened to, the other considering the comparatively new province of film scoring and its relation to the movie-goer. The first of these added sections needs a word of explanation in view of my orig-

*EDITOR'S NOTE: Translations of *What to Listen for in Music* have
appeared in German, Italian, Spanish, Swedish, Hebrew, and Persian.

Author's Note

inal claim, in the Preface to the first edition, that contemporary composition posed no special listening problems of its own. This still seems to me to be true. Nevertheless, it is equally true that after fifty years of so-called modern music there are still thousands of well-intentioned music lovers who think it sounds peculiar. It seemed worth an extra try to see if I could elucidate some few facets of new music listening that do not come within the scope of other chapters. Both new sections are based on articles originally prepared for *The New York Times Magazine*. My thanks are due the editors for permission to recast some of the material originally printed there.

At the back of the book a list of recordings of works mentioned in the text (with a few additions) will be found. For those interested in further reading, a short bibliography has been added, including a special listing of books by composer-authors. These were set down in the hope that listeners would want to hear composers speak for themselves.

Aaron Copland
CROTONVILLE, NEW YORK

Preface

T O PUT down as clearly as possible the fundamentals of intelligent music listening is the object of this book. The job of "explaining" music is no easy one, and I cannot flatter myself that I have succeeded better than others. But most writers on music appreciation approach the problem from the standpoint of the educator or the music critic. This is a composer's book.

Preface

To a composer, listening to music is a perfectly natural and simple process. That's what it should be for others. If there is any explaining to be done, the composer naturally thinks that, since he knows what goes into a musical composition, none has a better right to say what the listener ought to get from it.

Perhaps the composer is wrong about that. Perhaps the creative artist cannot be so objective in his approach to music as the more detached educator. But it seems to me that the risk is worth taking. For the composer has something vital at stake. In helping others to hear music more intelligently, he is working toward the spread of a musical culture, which in the end will affect the understanding of his own creations.

Still the question remains, how to go about it? How can the professional composer break down the barrier between himself and the lay listener? What can the composer say to make music more completely the listener's own? This book is an attempt to answer these questions.

Given the chance, every composer would like to know two very important things about anyone who takes himself seriously as a music lover. He would like to know these two things:

1. Are you hearing everything that is going on?
2. Are you really being sensitive to it?

Preface

Or, to put it differently:

1. Are you missing anything as far as the notes themselves are concerned?

2. Is your reaction a confused one, or are you quite clarified as to your emotional response?

Those are very pertinent questions, no matter what the music may be. They apply equally well to a Palestrina Mass, a Balinese gamelin, a Chávez sonatina, or the *Fifth Symphony*. In fact, they are the very same questions that the composer puts to himself, more or less consciously, whenever he is confronted with unfamiliar music, old or new. For, after all, there is nothing infallible about a composer's musical instincts. The main difference between him and the lay listener is that he is better prepared to listen.

This book, then, is a preparation for listening.

No composer worthy of the name would be content to prepare you to listen only to music of the past. That is why I have tried to apply every point made not only to established master works but also to the music of living men. I have often observed that the mark of a real music lover was an imperious desire to become familiar with every manifestation of the art, ancient and modern. Real lovers of music are unwilling to have their musical enjoyment confined to the overworked period of the three B's. The reader, on the other hand, may think that he has accomplished enough if he has been led to a richer understanding of the accepted classics. But it is my belief that the "problem" of listening to a fugue by Handel is essentially no different from that of listening to a similar work by Hindemith. There is a definite similarity of procedure which it would be foolish to ignore, quite aside from the question of relative merit. Inasmuch as I am bound to discuss fugues in a book of this kind, the reader might just as well see the fugue form exemplified in a new work as in an old one.

Unfortunately, whether the music is old or new, a certain number of technicalities have to be explained. Otherwise the reader cannot hope to grasp explanations of the higher musical forms. In every instance I have made an effort to keep technicalities to a minimum. It has always seemed to me more important for the listener to be sensitive to the musical tone than to know the number of vibrations that produce the tone. Information of that kind is of limited value even to the composer himself. What he desires above all is to encourage you to become as completely conscious and wideawake a listener as can possibly be developed. There lies the kernel of the problem of understanding music. It is no more difficult than that.

Though the book was written primarily with the lay-

Preface

man in mind, it is my hope that music students may also profit by reading it. In their concentration on perfecting themselves in the particular piece they happen to be studying, typical conservatory students tend to lose sight of the art of music as a whole. This book may serve, perhaps, especially in the later chapters on fundamental forms, to crystallize the loose general knowledge the student often acquires.

No solution has been found for the perennial problem of supplying satisfactory musical examples. Every piece of music mentioned in the text has been recorded and therefore may be heard by the reader. For the benefit of quick reference by those who read notes, a moderate number of musical illustrations have been printed in the text. Some day the perfect method for illustrating a book's statement about music may be discovered. Until then, the unfortunate layman will have to accept a number of my observations on simple faith.

Acknowledgments

WHAT TO LISTEN FOR IN MUSIC was the title of a course of fifteen lectures given by the author at the New School for Social Research in New York City during the winters of 1936 and 1937. Dr. Alvin Johnson, director of the New School, deserves my thanks for providing the public forum which stimulated the writing of this book.

The talks were designed for the layman and music student, not for the professional musician. The present volume, therefore, is correspondingly limited in scope. My purpose was not to be all-inclusive on a subject that might very easily spread itself but to confine the discussion to what seemed to me to be essential listening problems.

The manuscript was read by Mr. Elliott Carter, to whom I am indebted for valuable suggestions and friendly criticisms.

What to Listen for in Music

I

Preliminaries

ALL books on understanding music are agreed about one point: You can't develop a better appreciation of the art merely by reading a book about it. If you want to understand music better, you can do nothing more important than listen to it. Nothing can possibly take the place of listening to music. Everything that I have to say in this book is said about an experience that you can only get outside this book.

Therefore, you will probably be wasting your time in reading it unless you make a firm resolve to hear a great deal more music than you have in the past. All of us, professionals and nonprofessionals, are forever trying to deepen our understanding of the art. Reading a book may sometimes help us. But nothing can replace the prime consideration—listening to music itself.

Luckily, opportunities for hearing music are much greater than they ever were before. With the increasing availability of good music on radio and phonograph, not to mention television and the movies, almost anybody has the chance to listen to music. In fact, as a friend of mine recently said, nowadays everybody has the chance *not* to understand music.

It has often seemed to me that there is a tendency to exaggerate the difficulty of properly understanding music. We musicians are constantly meeting some honest soul who invariably says, in one form or another: "I love music very much, but I don't understand anything about it." My playwright and novelist friends rarely hear anyone say, "I don't understand anything about the theater or the novel." Yet I strongly suspect that those very same people, so modest about music, have just as much reason to be modest about the other arts. Or, to put it more graciously, have just as little reason

Preliminaries

to be modest about their understanding of music. If you have any feelings of inferiority about your musical reactions, try to rid yourself of them. They are often not justified.

At any rate, you have no reason to be downcast about your musical capacities until you have some idea of what it means to be musical. There are many strange popular notions as to what "being musical" consists of. One is always being told, as the unarguable proof of a musical person, that he or she can "go to a show and then come home and play all the tunes on the piano." That fact alone bespeaks a certain musicality in the person in question, but it does not indicate the kind of sensitivity to music that is under examination here. The entertainer who mimics well is not yet an actor, and the musical mimic is not necessarily a profoundly musical individual. Another attribute which is trotted forth whenever the question of being musical arises is that of having absolute pitch. To be able to recognize the note A when you hear it may, at times, be helpful, but it certainly does not prove, taken by itself, that you are a musical person. It should not be taken to indicate anything more than a glib musicality which has only a limited significance in relationship to the real understanding of music which concerns us here.

[5]

What to Listen for in Music

There is, however, one minimum requirement for the potentially intelligent listener. He must be able to recognize a melody when he hears it. If there is such a thing as being tone-deaf, then it suggests the inability to recognize a tune. Such a person has my sympathy, but he cannot be helped; just as the color-blind are a useless lot to the painter.* But if you feel confident that you can recognize a given melody—not *sing* a melody, but recognize it when played, even after an interval of a few minutes and after other and different melodies have been sounded—the key to a deeper appreciation of music is in your hands.

It is insufficient merely to hear music in terms of the separate moments at which it exists. You must be able to relate what you hear at any given moment to what has just happened before and what is about to come afterward. In other words, music is an art that exists in point of time. In that sense it is like a novel, except that the events of a novel are easier to keep in mind, partly because real happenings are narrated and partly because one can turn back and refresh one's memory of them. Musical "events" are more abstract by nature, so that the act of pulling them all together

---

*William Schuman contests this statement. As a result of practical work with amateurs he claims good results in aiding those previously held tone-deaf to recognize melodic materials.

in the imagination is not so easy as in reading a novel. That is why it is necessary for you to be able to recognize a tune. For the thing that takes the place of a story in music is, as a rule, the melody. The melody is generally what guides the listener. If you can't recognize a melody on its first appearance and can't follow its peregrinations straight through to its final appearance, I fail to see what you have to go on in listening. You are just vaguely being aware of the music. But recognizing a tune means you know where you are in the music and have a good chance of knowing where you're going. It is the only *sine qua non* of a more intelligent approach to understanding music.

Certain schools of thought are inclined to stress the value for the listener of some practical experience of music. They say, in effect, play *Old Black Joe* on the piano with one finger and it will get you closer to the mysteries of music than reading a dozen volumes. No harm can come, certainly, from pecking the piano a bit or even from playing it moderately well. But as an introduction to music I am suspicious of it, if only because of the many pianists who spend their lives playing great works, yet whose understanding of music is, on the whole, rather weak. As for the popularizers, who first began by attaching flowery stories and descriptive titles to make music easier and ended by adding doggerel

[7]

to themes from famous compositions—their "solution" for the listener's problems is beneath contempt.

No composer believes that there are any short cuts to the better appreciation of music. The only thing that one can do for the listener is to point out what actually exists in the music itself and reasonably to explain the wherefore and the why of the matter. The listener must do the rest.

2

How We Listen

WE ALL listen to music according to our separate
capacities. But, for the sake of analysis, the
whole listening process may become clearer if we break
it up into its component parts, so to speak. In a certain
sense we all listen to music on three separate planes. For
lack of a better terminology, one might name these:
(1) the sensuous plane, (2) the expressive plane, (3) the
sheerly musical plane. The only advantage to be gained

from mechanically splitting up the listening process into these hypothetical planes is the clearer view to be had of the way in which we listen.

The simplest way of listening to music is to listen for the sheer pleasure of the musical sound itself. That is the sensuous plane. It is the plane on which we hear music without thinking, without considering it in any way. One turns on the radio while doing something else and absent-mindedly bathes in the sound. A kind of brainless but attractive state of mind is engendered by the mere sound appeal of the music.

You may be sitting in a room reading this book. Imagine one note struck on the piano. Immediately that one note is enough to change the atmosphere of the room—proving that the sound element in music is a powerful and mysterious agent, which it would be foolish to deride or belittle.

The surprising thing is that many people who consider themselves qualified music lovers abuse that plane in listening. They go to concerts in order to lose themselves. They use music as a consolation or an escape. They enter an ideal world where one doesn't have to think of the realities of everyday life. Of course they aren't thinking about the music either. Music allows them to leave it, and they go off to a place to dream, dreaming because of and apropos of the music yet never quite listening to it.

Yes, the sound appeal of music is a potent and primitive force, but you must not allow it to usurp a disproportionate share of your interest. The sensuous plane is an important one in music, a very important one, but it does not constitute the whole story.

There is no need to digress further on the sensuous plane. Its appeal to every normal human being is self-evident. There is, however, such a thing as becoming more sensitive to the different kinds of sound stuff as used by various composers. For all composers do not use that sound stuff in the same way. Don't get the idea that the value of music is commensurate with its sensuous appeal or that the loveliest sounding music is made by the greatest composer. If that were so, Ravel would be a greater creator than Beethoven. The point is that the sound element varies with each composer, that his usage of sound forms an integral part of his style and must be taken into account when listening. The reader can see, therefore, that a more conscious approach is valuable even on this primary plane of music listening.

The second plane on which music exists is what I have called the expressive one. Here, immediately, we tread on controversial ground. Composers have a way of shying away from any discussion of music's expressive side. Did not Stravinsky himself proclaim that his music was an "object," a "thing," with a life of its own, and with no other meaning than its own purely musical existence? This intransigent attitude of Stravinsky's may be due to the fact that so many people have tried to read different meanings into so many pieces. Heaven knows it is difficult enough to say precisely what it is that a piece of music means, to say it definitely, to say it finally so that everyone is satisfied with your explanation. But that should not lead one to the other extreme of denying to music the right to be "expressive."

My own belief is that all music has an expressive power, some more and some less, but that all music has a certain meaning behind the notes and that the meaning behind the notes constitutes, after all, what the piece is saying, what the piece is about. This whole problem can be stated quite simply by asking, "Is there a meaning to music?" My answer to that would be, "Yes." And "Can you state in so many words what the meaning is?" My answer to that would be, "No." Therein lies the difficulty.

Simple-minded souls will never be satisfied with the answer to the second of these questions. They always

How We Listen

want music to have a meaning, and the more concrete it is the better they like it. The more the music reminds them of a train, a storm, a funeral, or any other familiar conception the more expressive it appears to be to them. This popular idea of music's meaning—stimulated and abetted by the usual run of musical commentator—should be discouraged wherever and whenever it is met. One timid lady once confessed to me that she suspected something seriously lacking in her appreciation of music because of her inability to connect it with anything definite. That is getting the whole thing backward, of course.

Still, the question remains, How close should the intelligent music lover wish to come to pinning a definite meaning to any particular work? No closer than a general concept, I should say. Music expresses, at different moments, serenity or exuberance, regret or triumph, fury or delight. It expresses each of these moods, and many others, in a numberless variety of subtle shadings and differences. It may even express a state of meaning for which there exists no adequate word in any language. In that case, musicians often like to say that it has only a purely musical meaning. They sometimes go farther and say that *all* music has only a purely musical meaning. What they really mean is that no appropriate word can be found to express the music's meaning and that, even if it could, they do not feel the need of finding it.

But whatever the professional musician may hold, most musical novices still search for specific words with which to pin down their musical reactions. That is why they always find Tschaikovsky easier to "understand" than Beethoven. In the first place, it is easier to pin a meaning-word on a Tschaikovsky piece than on a Beethoven one. Much easier. Moreover, with the Russian composer, every time you come back to a piece of his it almost always says the same thing to you, whereas with Beethoven it is often quite difficult to put your finger right on what he is saying. And any musician will tell you that that is why Beethoven is the greater composer. Because music which always says the same thing to you will necessarily soon become dull music, but music whose meaning is slightly different with each hearing has a greater chance of remaining alive.

Listen, if you can, to the forty-eight fugue themes of Bach's *Well Tempered Clavichord*. Listen to each theme, one after another. You will soon realize that each theme mirrors a different world of feeling. You will also soon realize that the more beautiful a theme seems to you the harder it is to find any word that will describe it to your complete satisfaction. Yes, you will certainly know whether it is a gay theme or a sad one. You will be able, in other words, in your own mind, to draw a frame of emotional feeling around your theme. Now study the sad one a little closer. Try to pin down the exact quality of its sadness. Is it pessimistically sad or resignedly sad; is it fatefully sad or smilingly sad?

Let us suppose that you are fortunate and can describe to your own satisfaction in so many words the exact meaning of your chosen theme. There is still no guarantee that anyone else will be satisfied. Nor need they be. The important thing is that each one feel for himself the specific expressive quality of a theme or, similarly, an entire piece of music. And if it is a great work of art, don't expect it to mean exactly the same thing to you each time you return to it.

Themes or pieces need not express only one emotion, of course. Take such a theme as the first main one of the *Ninth Symphony*, for example. It is clearly made up of different elements. It does not say only one thing. Yet anyone hearing it immediately gets a feeling of strength, a feeling of power. It isn't a power that comes simply because the theme is played loudly. It is a power inherent in the theme itself. The extraordinary strength and vigor of the theme results in the listener's receiving an impression that a forceful statement has been made. But one should never try to boil it down to "the fateful hammer of life," etc. That is where the trouble begins. The musician, in his exasperation, says it means nothing but the notes themselves, whereas the nonprofessional is only too anxious to hang on to any explanation that gives him the illusion of getting closer to the music's meaning.

Now, perhaps, the reader will know better what I mean when I say that music does have an expressive meaning but that we cannot say in so many words what that meaning is.

The third plane on which music exists is the sheerly musical plane. Besides the pleasurable sound of music and the expressive feeling that it gives off, music does exist in terms of the notes themselves and of their manipulation. Most listeners are not sufficiently conscious of this third plane. It will be largely the business of this book to make them more aware of music on this plane.

Professional musicians, on the other hand, are, if anything, too conscious of the mere notes themselves. They often fall into the error of becoming so engrossed with their arpeggios and staccatos that they forget the deeper aspects of the music they are performing. But from the layman's standpoint, it is not so much a matter of getting over bad habits on the sheerly musical plane as of increasing one's awareness of what is going on, in so far as the notes are concerned.

When the man in the street listens to the "notes themselves" with any degree of concentration, he is most likely to make some mention of the melody. Either he hears a pretty melody or he does not, and he generally lets it go at that. Rhythm is likely to gain his attention next, particularly if it seems exciting. But harmony and tone color are generally taken for granted, if they are thought of consciously at all. As for music's having a definite form of some kind, that idea seems never to have occurred to him.

It is very important for all of us to become more alive to music on its sheerly musical plane. After all, an actual musical material is being used. The intelligent listener must be prepared to increase his awareness of the musical material and what happens to it. He must hear the melodies, the rhythms, the harmonies, the tone colors in a more conscious fashion. But above all he must, in order to follow the line of the composer's thought, know something of the principles of musical form. Listening to all of these elements is listening on the sheerly musical plane.

Let me repeat that I have split up mechanically the three separate planes on which we listen merely for

the sake of greater clarity. Actually, we never listen
on one or the other of these planes. What we do is to
correlate them—listening in all three ways at the same
time. It takes no mental effort, for we do it instinctively.

Perhaps an analogy with what happens to us when
we visit the theater will make this instinctive correla-
tion clearer. In the theater, you are aware of the actors
and actresses, costumes and sets, sounds and movements. All these give one the sense that the theater is
a pleasant place to be in. They constitute the sensuous
plane in our theatrical reactions.

The expressive plane in the theater would be derived
from the feeling that you get from what is happening
on the stage. You are moved to pity, excitement, or
gayety. It is this general feeling, generated aside from
the particular words being spoken, a certain emotional
something which exists on the stage, that is analogous
to the expressive quality in music.

The plot and plot development is equivalent to our
sheerly musical plane. The playwright creates and develops a character in just the same way that a composer creates and develops a theme. According to the
degree of your awareness of the way in which the artist in either field handles his material will you become
a more intelligent listener.

How We Listen

It is easy enough to see that the theatergoer never is conscious of any of these elements separately. He is aware of them all at the same time. The same is true of music listening. We simultaneously and without thinking listen on all three planes.

In a sense, the ideal listener is both inside and outside the music at the same moment, judging it and enjoying it, wishing it would go one way and watching it go another—almost like the composer at the moment he composes it; because in order to write his music, the composer must also be inside and outside his music, carried away by it and yet coldly critical of it. A subjective and objective attitude is implied in both creating and listening to music.

What the reader should strive for, then, is a more *active* kind of listening. Whether you listen to Mozart or Duke Ellington, you can deepen your understanding of music only by being a more conscious and aware listener—not someone who is just listening, but someone who is listening *for* something.

3

The Creative Process in Music

Most people want to know how things are made. They frankly admit, however, that they feel completely at sea when it comes to understanding how a piece of music is made. Where a composer begins, how he manages to keep going—in fact, how and where he learns his trade—all are shrouded in impenetrable darkness. The composer, in short, is a man of mystery to most people, and the composer's workshop an unapproachable ivory tower.

[20]

The Creative Process in Music

One of the first things most people want to hear discussed in relation to composing is the question of inspiration. They find it difficult to believe that composers are not as preoccupied with that question as they had supposed. The layman always finds it hard to realize how natural it is for the composer to compose. He has a tendency to put himself into the position of the composer and to visualize the problems involved, including that of inspiration, from the perspective of the layman. He forgets that composing to a composer is like fulfilling a natural function. It is like eating or sleeping. It is something that the composer happens to have been born to do; and, because of that, it loses the character of a special virtue in the composer's eyes.

The composer, therefore, confronted with the question of inspiration, does not say to himself: "Do I feel inspired?" He says to himself: "Do I feel like composing today?" And if he feels like composing, he does. It is more or less like saying to yourself: "Do I feel sleepy?" If you feel sleepy, you go to sleep. If you don't feel sleepy, you stay up. If the composer doesn't feel like composing, he doesn't compose. It's as simple as that.

Of course, after you have finished composing, you hope that everyone, including yourself, will recognize the thing you have written as having been inspired. But that is really an idea tacked on at the end.

Someone once asked me, in a public forum, whether I waited for inspiration. My answer was: "Every day!" But that does not, by any means, imply a passive waiting around for the divine afflatus. That is exactly what separates the professional from the dilettante. The professional composer can sit down day after day and turn out some kind of music. On some days it will undoubtedly be better than on others; but the primary fact is the ability to compose. Inspiration is often only a by-product.

The second question that most people find intriguing is generally worded thus: "Do you or don't you write your music at the piano?" A current idea exists that there is something shameful about writing a piece of music at the piano. Along with that goes a mental picture of Beethoven composing out in the fields. Think about it a moment and you will realize that writing away from the piano nowadays is not nearly so simple a matter as it was in Mozart or Beethoven's day. For one thing, harmony is so much more complex than it was then. Few composers are capable of writing down entire compositions without at least a passing reference to the piano. In fact, Stravinsky in his *Autobiography* has even gone so far as to say that it is a bad thing to

The Creative Process in Music

write music away from the piano because the composer should always be in contact with *la matière sonore*. That's a violent taking of the opposite side. But, in the end, the way in which a composer writes is a personal matter. The method is unimportant. It is the result that counts.

The really important question is: "What does the composer start with; where does he begin?" The answer to that is, Every composer begins with a musical idea—a *musical* idea, you understand, not a mental, literary, or extramusical idea. Suddenly a theme comes to him. (Theme is used as synonymous with musical idea.) The composer starts with his theme; and the theme is a gift from Heaven. He doesn't know where it comes from—has no control over it. It comes almost like automatic writing. That's why he keeps a book very often and writes themes down whenever they come. He collects musical ideas. You can't do anything about that element of composing.

The idea itself may come in various forms. It may come as a melody—just a one-line simple melody which you might hum to yourself. Or it may come to the composer as a melody with an accompaniment. At times he may not even hear a melody; he may simply conceive an accompanimental figure to which a melody will probably be added later. Or, on the other hand, the theme may take the form of a purely rythmic idea. He hears a particular kind of drumbeat, and that will be enough to start him off. Over it he will soon begin hearing an accompaniment and melody. The original conception, however, was a mere rhythm. Or, a different type of composer may possibly begin with a contrapuntal web of two or three melodies which are heard at the same instant. That, however, is a less usual species of thematic inspiration.

All these are different ways in which the musical idea may present itself to the composer.

Now, the composer has the idea. He has a number of them in his book, and he examines them in more or less the way that you, the listener, would examine them if you looked at them. He wants to know what he has. He examines the musical line for its purely formal beauty. He likes to see the way it rises and falls, as if it were a drawn line instead of a musical one. He may even try to retouch it, just as you might in drawing a line, so that the rise and fall of the melodic contour might be improved.

But he also wants to know the emotional significance of his theme. If all music has expressive value, then the composer must become conscious of the expressive values of his theme. He may be unable to put it into so many words, but he feels it! He instinctively knows

[24]

whether he has a gay or a sad theme, a noble or dia-
bolic one. Sometimes he may be mystified himself as
to its exact quality. But sooner or later he will probably instinctively decide what the emotional nature of
his theme is, because that's the thing he is about to
work with.

Always remember that a theme is, after all, only a
succession of notes. Merely by changing the dynamics, that is, by playing it loudly and bravely or softly
and timidly, one can transform the emotional feeling
of the very same succession of notes. By a change of
harmony a new poignancy may be given the theme;
or by a different rhythmic treatment the same notes
may result in a war dance instead of a lullaby. Every
composer keeps in mind the possible metamorphoses
of his succession of notes. First he tries to find its essential nature, and then he tries to find what might be
done with it—how that essential nature may momentarily be changed.

As a matter of fact, the experience of most composers has been that the more complete a theme is the less
possibility there is of seeing it in various aspects. If
the theme itself, in its original form, is long enough
and complete enough, the composer may have difficulty in seeing it in any other way. It already exists in
its definitive form. That is why great music can be

written on themes that in themselves are insignificant. One might very well say that the less complete, the less important, the theme the more likely it is to be open to new connotations. Some of Bach's greatest organ fugues are constructed on themes that are comparatively uninteresting in themselves.

The current notion that all music is beautiful according to whether the theme is beautiful or not doesn't hold true in many cases. Certainly the composer does not judge his theme by that criterion alone.

Having looked at his thematic material, the composer must now decide what sound medium will best fit it. Is it a theme that belongs in a symphony, or does it seem more intimate in character and therefore better fitted for a string quartet? Is it a lyrical theme that would be used to best advantage in a song; or had it better be saved, because of its dramatic quality, for operatic treatment? A composer sometimes has a work half finished before he understands the medium for which it is best fitted.

Thus far I have been presupposing an abstract composer before an abstract theme. But actually I can see three different types of composers in musical history, each of whom conceives music in a somewhat different fashion.

The type that has fired public imagination most is

that of the spontaneously inspired composer—the Franz Schubert type, in other words. All composers are inspired of course, but this type is more spontaneously inspired. Music simply wells out of him. He can't get it down on paper fast enough. You can almost always tell this type of composer by his prolific output. In certain months, Schubert wrote a song a day. Hugo Wolf did the same.

In a sense, men of this kind begin not so much with a musical theme as with a completed composition. They invariably work best in the shorter forms. It is much easier to improvise a song than it is to improvise a symphony. It isn't easy to be inspired in that spontaneous way for long periods at a stretch. Even Schubert was more successful in handling the shorter forms of music. The spontaneously inspired man is only one type of composer, with his own limitations.

Beethoven symbolizes the second type—the constructive type, one might call it. This type exemplifies my theory of the creative process in music better than any other, because in this case the composer really does begin with a musical theme. In Beethoven's case there is no doubt about it, for we have the notebooks in which he put the themes down. We can see from his notebooks how he worked over his themes—how he would not let them be until they were as perfect as he

[27]

could make them. Beethoven was not a spontaneously inspired composer in the Schubert sense at all. He was the type that begins with a theme; makes it a germinal idea; and upon that constructs a musical work, day after day, in painstaking fashion. Most composers since Beethoven's day belong to this second type.

The third type of creator I can only call, for lack of a better name, the traditionalist type. Men like Palestrina and Bach belong in this category. They both exemplify the kind of composer who is born in a particular period of musical history, when a certain musical style is about to reach its fullest development. It is a question at such a time of creating music in a well-known and accepted style and doing it in a way that is better than anyone has done it before you.

Beethoven and Schubert started from a different premise. They both had serious pretensions to originality! After all, Schubert practically created the song form singlehanded; and the whole face of music changed after Beethoven lived. But Bach and Palestrina simply improved on what had gone before them.

The traditionalist type of composer begins with a pattern rather than with a theme. The creative act with Palestrina is not the thematic conception so much as the personal treatment of a well-established pattern. And even Bach, who conceived forty-eight of the most varied and inspired themes in his *Well Tempered Clav-ichord*, knew in advance the general formal mold that they were to fill. It goes without saying that we are not living in a traditionalist period nowadays.

One might add, for the sake of completeness, a fourth type of composer—the pioneer type: men like Gesualdo in the seventeenth century, Moussorgsky and Berlioz in the nineteenth, Debussy and Edgar Varese in the twentieth. It is difficult to summarize the composing methods of so variegated a group. One can safely say that their approach to composition is the opposite of the traditionalist type. They clearly oppose conventional solutions of musical problems. In many ways, their attitude is experimental—they seek to add new harmonies, new sonorities, new formal principles. The pioneer type was the characteristic one at the turn of the seventeenth century and also at the beginning of the twentieth century, but it is much less evident today.*

But let's return to our theoretical composer. We have him with his idea—his musical idea—with some conception of its expressive nature, with a sense of what can be done with it, and with a preconceived notion of what medium is best fitted for it. Still he hasn't a

---

*Recent experiments with electronically produced music, however, point to a new species of scientifically trained composer as the pioneer type of our own time.

piece. A musical idea is not the same as a piece of music. It only induces a piece of music. The composer knows very well that something else is needed in order to create the finished composition.

He tries, first of all, to find other ideas that seem to go with the original one. They may be ideas of a similar character, or they may be contrasting ones. These additional ideas will probably not be so important as the one that came first—usually they play a subsidiary role. Yet they definitely seem necessary in order to complete the first one. Still that's not enough! Some way must be found for getting from one idea to the next, and it is generally achieved through use of so-called bridge material.

There are also two other important ways in which the composer can add to his original material. One is the elongation process. Often the composer finds that a particular theme needs elongating so that its character may be more clearly defined. Wagner was a master at elongation. I referred to the other way when I visualized the composer's examining the possible metamorphoses of his theme. That is the much written-about development of his material, which is a very important part of his job.

All these things are necessary for the creation of a full-sized piece—the germinal idea, the addition of other lesser

The Creative Process in Music

ideas, the elongation of the ideas, the bridge material for the connection of the ideas, and their full development.

Now comes the most difficult task of all—the welding together of all that material so that it makes a coherent whole. In the finished product, everything must be in its place. The listener must be able to find his way around in the piece. There should be no possible chance of his confusing the principal theme with the bridge material, or vice versa. The composition must have a beginning, a middle, and an end; and it is up to the composer to see to it that the listener always has some sense of where he is in relation to beginning, middle, and end. Moreover, the whole thing should be managed artfully so that none can say where the soldering began—where the composer's spontaneous invention left off and the hard work began.

Of course, I do not mean to suggest that in putting his materials together the composer necessarily begins from scratch. On the contrary, every well-trained composer has, as his stock in trade, certain normal structural molds on which to lean for the basic framework of his compositions. These formal molds I speak of have all been gradually evolved over hundreds of years as the combined efforts of numberless composers seeking a way to ensure the coherence of their compositions. What these forms are and exactly in what manner the composer depends on them will materialize in later chapters.

But whatever the form the composer chooses to adopt, there is always one great desideratum: The form must have what in my student days we used to call *la grande ligne* (the long line). It is difficult adequately to explain the meaning of that phrase to the layman. To be properly understood in relation to a piece of music, it must be felt. In mere words, it simply means that every good piece of music must give us a sense of flow—a sense of continuity from first note to last. Every elementary music student knows the principle, but to put it into practice has challenged the greatest minds in music! A great symphony is a man-made Mississippi down which we irresistibly flow from the instant of our leave-taking to a long foreseen destination. Music must always flow, for that is part of its very essence, but the creation of that continuity and flow—that long line—constitutes the be-all and end-all of every composer's existence.

4

The Four Elements of Music

I · RHYTHM

M USIC has four essential elements: rhythm, melody, harmony, and tone color. These four ingredients are the composer's materials. He works with them in the same way that any other artisan works with his materials. From the standpoint of the lay listener they have only a limited value, for he is seldom conscious of hearing any one of them separately. It is their combined effect—the seemingly inextricable web of

[33]

sound that they form—with which listeners are concerned for the most part.

Still, the layman will find that it is well-nigh impossible to have a fuller conception of musical content without in some degree delving into the intricacies of rhythm, melody, harmony, and tone color. A complete understanding of the separate elements belongs with the deepest technicalities of the art. In a book of this kind, only so much information should be imparted as will help the listener more exactly to grasp the effect of the whole. Some knowledge of the historical development of these primary elements is also necessary if the reader is to arrive at a more just view of the relationship of contemporary music to the art of the past.

Most historians agree that if music started anywhere, it started with the beating of a rhythm. An unadulterated rhythm is so immediate and direct in its effect upon us that we instinctively feel its primal origins. If we had any reason for suspecting our instinct in the matter, we could always turn to the music of savage tribes for verification. Today, as ever, it is music almost entirely of rhythm alone and often of an astonishing complexity. Not only the testimony of music itself but the close relationship of certain patterns of doing work to rhythmic patterns, and the natural tie-

Rhythm

up between bodily movement and basic rhythms are further proof, if proof were needed, that rhythm is the first of the musical elements.

Many thousands of years were to pass before man learned how to write down the rhythms that he played or those that he sang in later ages. Even today our system of rhythmic notation is far from perfect. We still are unable to note down subtle differences such as every accomplished artist instinctively adds in performance. But our system, with its regular division of rhythmic units into measures separated by bar lines, is adequate for most purposes.

When musical rhythm was first put down, it was not measured off into evenly distributed metrical units as it now is. It wasn't until about 1150 that "measured music," as it was then called, was slowly introduced into Western civilization. There are two opposing ways in which one might regard this revolutionary change, for it had both a liberating and a restraining effect on music.

Up until that time, much of the music of which we have any record was vocal music; it invariably accompanied prose or poetry as a modest handmaiden. From the time of the Greeks to the full flowering of Gregorian chant, the rhythm of music was the natural, unfettered rhythm of prose or poetic speech. No one then, or since, has ever been able to write down that kind of rhythm with any degree of exactitude. Monsieur Jourdain, the protagonist of Molière's comedy, would have been doubly astonished if he had known that he was not only talking prose but that his prose rhythm was of a subtlety that defied transcribing.

The first rhythms that were successfully transcribed were of a much more regulated character. This innovation gradually had many and far-reaching effects. It helped considerably to divorce music from its dependence on the word; it supplied music with a rhythmic structure of its own; it made possible the exact reproduction of the composer's rhythmical conceptions from generation to generation; but, most of all, it was responsible for the subsequent contrapuntal, or many-voiced, music, unthinkable without measured metrical units. It would be difficult to exaggerate the inventive genius of those who first developed rhythmical notation. Yet it would be foolish to underestimate the confining influence that it has had on our rhythmical imagination, particularly at certain periods of musical history. How this came about we shall soon see.

The reader may be wondering by this time what, musically speaking, we mean by "measured metrical units." Almost everyone, at some time in his life, has

Rhythm

marched in a parade. The footbeats themselves seem to call out: LEFT, right, LEFT, right; or ONE, two, ONE, two; or, to put it into simplest musical termi-

nology: 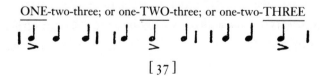 That is one meas-

ured metrical unit of 2/4 time. One could continue beating out this same metrical unit for a few minutes, as children sometimes do, and have the basic rhythmic pattern of any march. The same holds true for the other

basic metrical unit by threes: which is

a measure of 3/4 time. If the first of these rhythms is doubled, we get a measure of 4/4 time, thus: ONE-two-THREE-four; if the second is doubled, we get 6/4 time: ONE-two-three-FOUR-five-six. In these simple units, the stress, or accent, as we call it in music (marked >), normally falls on the first beat of each measure. But the accented note need not necessarily be the first of each measure. As an example, take a measure of 3/4 time. There is the possibility of accenting not only the first beat but also the second or the third, thus:

The second two are examples of irregular, or displaced, accents in 3/4 time.

The fascination and emotional impact of simple rhythms such as these, repeated over and over again, as they sometimes are, with electrifying effect, is quite beyond analysis. All we can do is humbly to acknowledge their powerful and often hypnotic effect upon us and not feel quite so superior to the savage tribesman who first discovered them.

Such simple rhythms, however, carry with them the danger of monotony, particularly as used by so-called "art" composers. Nineteenth-century composers, primarily interested in extending the harmonic language of music, allowed their sense of rhythm to become dulled by an overdose of regularly recurring downbeats. Even the greatest of them are open to this accusation. That probably is the origin for the conception of rhythm entertained by the ordinary music teacher of the past generation who taught that the first beat of every metrical unit is *always* the strong one.

There is, of course, a much richer conception of rhythmic life than that, even as applied to nineteenth-century classics. In order to explain what it is, it is necessary to make clear the distinction between meter and rhythm.

Rhythm

Properly understood, there is seldom in art music a rhythmic scheme that is not made up of these two factors: meter and rhythm. To the layman, unfamiliar with musical terminology, any confusion between the two can be avoided by keeping in mind a similar situation in poetry. When we scan a line of verse, we are merely measuring its metrical units, just as we do in music when we divide the notes into evenly distributed note values. In neither case do we have the rhythm of the phrase. Thus, if we recite the following line, stressing the regular beats of the metrical line, we get:

What is your substance, whereof are you made,

That millions of strange shadows on you tend?

Reading it thus, we get only its syllable sense, not its rhythmic sense. Rhythm comes only when we read it for its meaning sense.

Similarly in music, when we stress the down beat: ONE-two-three; ONE-two-three; and so forth, as some of us were taught to do by our teachers, we get only the meter. We get the real rhythm only when we stress the notes according to the musical sense of the phrase. The difference between music and poetry is that in music a sense of both meter and rhythm may be more obviously present at the same time. Even in a simple piano piece there is a left hand and a right hand at work at the same time. Often the left hand does little more, rhythmically speaking, than play an accompaniment in which the meter and rhythm exactly coincide, while the right hand moves freely within and around the metrical unit without ever stressing it. An especially fine example of that is the slow movement of Bach's *Italian Concerto*. Schumann and Brahms also supply numerous examples of the subtle interplay of meter and rhythm.

Toward the end of the nineteenth century, the humdrum regularity of metrical units of twos and threes and their multiples began to be broken up. Instead of writing an unvarying rhythm of ONE-two, ONE-two; or ONE-two-three, ONE-two-three, we find Tschaikovsky, in the second movement of his *Pathetic Symphony*, venturing a rhythm made up of a combination of the two: ONE-two-ONE-two-three, ONE-two-ONE-two-three. Or, to put it more exactly: ONE-two-THREE-four-five, ONE-two-THREE-four-five. Tschaikovsky, no doubt, like other Russian composers of his time, was only borrowing from Russian folk-song sources when he introduced this unusual meter. Wherever it came from, our

Rhythm

rhythmic schemes have never been the same since that time.

But the Russian composer had only taken a first step. Though beginning with an unconventional rhythm in five, he nevertheless kept it rigorously throughout the movement. It was left for Stravinsky to draw the inevitable conclusion of writing changing meters with every bar. Such a procedure looks something like this: ONE-two, ONE-two-three, ONE-two-three, ONE-two, ONE-two-three-four, ONE-two-three, ONE-two, etc. Now read that in strict tempo and as fast as you can. You will see why musicians found Stravinsky so difficult to perform when he was new. Also, why many people found these new rhythms so disconcerting merely to listen to. Without them, however, it is hard to see how Stravinsky could have achieved those jagged and uncouth rhythmic effects that first brought him fame.

At the same time, a new freedom developed within the confines of a single bar. It should be explained that in our system of rhythmic notation the following arbitrary note values are used: whole note ○ ; half note ♩ ; quarter note ♩ ; eighth note ♪ ; sixteenth note ♪ ; thirty-second note ♪ ; sixty-fourth note ♪ . In duration of time, a whole note would be the equivalent of two half notes, or four quarter notes, or eight eighth notes, and so forth, thus:

The time value of a whole note is only relative; that is to say, it may last two seconds or twenty seconds according to whether the tempo is fast or slow. But in every case, the smaller values into which it may be divided are exact divisions. In other words, if a whole note has a duration of four seconds, the four quarter notes into which it may be divided will have a value of one second each. In our system, it is customary to gather the notes into bars or measures. When there are four quarter notes in each measure, as is often the case, the piece is said to be in four-quarter time. This, of course, means that four quarters or their equivalent, such as two half notes or one whole note, will make up one bar. When a measure of four-quarter time is split up into eighth notes, the normal way of dividing them would be to group them by twos: 2–2–2–2.

Modern composers had the not unnatural idea of breaking the quarters into an unequal distribution of eighth notes, thus: or:

 The number of eighths remains the same, but their arrangement is no longer 2–2–2–2– but 3–2–3 or 2–3–3 or 3–3–2. Continuing this principle, composers soon were writing similar rhythms outside the bar line, making their rhythms look like this on the page: 2–3–3–2–4–3–2–etc.

This was another way, in other words, of achieving that same independence of rhythm that Stravinsky deduced from Russian folk song, via Tschaikovsky, Moussorgsky, *et al.*

Most musicians still find it easier to play a rhythm of 6/8 than one of 5/8, particularly in fast tempo. And most listeners feel more "comfortable" in the well-grooved, time-honored rhythms that they have always heard. But both musicians and listeners should be warned that the end of modern rhythmical experiments is not yet in sight.

The next step has already been taken—an even more complex stage of rhythmic development. It was brought about by the combination of two or more independent rhythms at the same time. These result in what has been termed polyrhythms.

The first polyrhythmic stage is simple enough and was often used by "classical" composers. When we were taught to play two against three or three against four or five against three, we were already playing polyrhythms, with the significant limitation that the first beat of each rhythm always coincided. In such cases, we get:

Right hand	1 – 2	1 – 2	or	Right hand	1 – 2 – 3	1 – 2 – 3
Left hand	1–2–3	1–2–3		Left hand	1–2–3–4	1–2–3–4

But it is two or more rhythms with first beats that do *not* coincide that really make for exciting and fascinating rhythms.

Don't imagine for an instant that such rhythmic complexities were unknown until our own time. On the contrary, by comparison with the intricate rhythms used by African drummers or Chinese or Hindu percussionists, we are mere neophytes. A real Cuban rhumba band, to come nearer home, can also show us a thing or two when it comes to the hectic use of polyrhythms. Our own "swing" bands, inspired by darker days of "hot jazz," also occasionally let loose a welter of polyrhythms which defy analysis.

Rhythm

Polyrhythms may be examined in their most elementary form in any simple jazz arrangement. Remember that really independent polyrhythms result only when down beats do *not* coincide. In such cases, a rhythm of two against three would look like this:

$$\frac{1-2-3-1-2-3}{1-2-1-2-1-2}$$

or, in musical terms:

All jazz is founded on the rock of a steady, unchanging rhythm in the bass. When jazz was only ragtime, the basic rhythm was merely that of march time: ONE-two-THREE-four, ONE-two-THREE-four. This same rhythm was made much more interesting in jazz by simply displacing the accents so that the basic rhythm became one-TWO-three-FOUR, one-TWO-three-FOUR. Unsuspecting citizens who object to the "monotony" of jazz rhythm unknowingly admit that all they hear is this foundational rhythm. But over and above it are other, and freer, rhythms; and it is the combination of the two that gives jazz whatever rhythmic vitality it possesses. I do not mean to say that all jazz music is continually and throughout each piece polyrhythmic but only that at its best moments it partakes of a true independence of different rhythms sounded simultaneously. One of the ear-

[45]

liest examples of these polyrhythms used in jazz will be found in the late George Gershwin's appropriately named *Fascinating Rhythm.**

Gershwin, in a commercial product, could use this device only sparingly. But Stravinsky, Bartók, Milhaud, and other modern composers had no such limitations. In works like the *Story of a Soldier* (Stravinsky) or the later Bartók string quartets, there are abundant examples of multiple rhythms logically carried out, producing unexpected and new-sounding rhythmic combinations.

Some of my more informed readers may be wondering why I have made no mention, in this outline of rhythmic development, of that phenomenal school of English composers who flourished in Shakespeare's day.

*Copyright Dec. 12, 1924, by Harms, Inc. Used by permission.

Rhythm

They wrote hundreds of madrigals which are overrun with the most ingenious of polyrhythms. Since they composed music for voices, their use of rhythm takes its being from the natural prosody of the words. And since each separate voice has its own separate part, the result makes for an unprecedented interweaving of independent rhythms. The characteristic feature of the rhythm of the madrigal composers is the lack of any sense of strong down beat. Because of that, later generations with less of a feeling for subtle rhythms accused the madrigalist school of being arrhythmic. This lack of a strong down beat makes the music look like this:

$$\frac{1-2-3-1-2-3-4}{\frac{1-2-1-2-3-1-2}{1-2-3-1-2-1}}$$

The effect is anything but primitive. Therein lies its main difference from the modern brand of polyrhythm, which depends for its effect upon an insistence on juxtaposed down beats.

No one can say where this new rhythmic freedom will take us. Already certain theorists have mathematically computed rhythmic combinations as possibilities that no composer has yet heard. "Paper rhythms" these may be called.

What to Listen for in Music

The lay listener is asked to remember that even the most complex rhythms were meant for his ears. They need not be analyzed to be enjoyed. All you need do is to relax, letting the rhythm do with you what it will. You already allow just that with simple and familiar rhythms. Later on, by listening more intently and not resisting the rhythmic pull in any way, the greater complexities of modern rhythm and the subtle rhythmic interplay of the madrigal school will undoubtedly add new interest to your music listening.

5

The Four Elements of Music

II · MELODY

MELODY is only second in importance to rhythm in the musical firmament. As one commentator has pointed out, if the idea of rhythm is connected in our imagination with physical motion, the idea of melody is associated with mental emotion. The effect upon us of both these primary elements is equally mysterious. Why a good melody should have the power to move us has thus far defied all analysis. We cannot even

[49]

say, with any degree of surety, what constitutes a good melody.

Still, most people think they know a beautiful melody when they hear one. Therefore, they must be applying certain criteria, even though unconscious ones. Though we may not be able to define what a good melody is in advance, we certainly can make some generalizations about melodies that we already know to be good, and that may help to make clearer characteristics of good melodic writing.

In writing music, a composer is forever accepting or rejecting melodies that come to him spontaneously. In no other department of composition is he forced to rely to the same extent on his musical instinct for guidance. But if he should attempt to work over a melody, there is every likelihood that he will bring to bear the same criteria that we use in judging it. What are some principles of sound melodic construction?

A beautiful melody, like a piece of music in its entirety, should be of satisfying proportions. It must give us a sense of completion and of inevitability. To do that, the melodic line will generally be long and flowing, with low and high points of interest and a climactic moment usually near the end. Obviously, such a melody would tend to move about among a variety of notes, avoiding unnecessary repetitions. A sensitivity

Melody

to rhythmic flow is also important in melodic construction. Many a fine melody has been made by some slight rhythmic change. But, most important of all, its expressive quality must be such as will arouse an emotional response in the listener. That is the most unpredictable attribute of all, for which no guiding rules exist. As far as mere construction goes, every good melody will be found to possess a skeletal frame which can be deduced from essential points in the melodic line after "unessential" notes have been pared away. Only a professional musician is capable of X-raying the melodic spine of a well-constructed melody, but the untutored layman can be depended upon to sense unconsciously the lack of a real melodic backbone. Such an analysis will generally show that melodies, like sentences, often have halfway stopping places, the equivalent of commas, semicolons, and colons in writing. These temporary resting points, or cadences as they are sometimes called, help to make the melodic line more intelligible, by dividing it into more easily understood phrases.

From a purely technical standpoint, all melodies exist within the limits of some scale system. A scale is nothing more than a certain arrangement of a particular series of notes. Investigation has shown that these "arrangements," so-called, are not arbitrary ones but have their justification in physical facts. The builders of scales relied on their instinct, and the men of science now back them up with their figures of relative vibrations to the second.

There have been four main systems of scale building: Oriental, Greek, Ecclesiastical, and Modern. For all practical purposes, we can say that most scale systems are based on a chosen number of notes between a given tone and its octave. In our modern system, this octave span is divided into twelve "equal" tones, called semitones, and together they comprise the chromatic scale. Most of our music is *not* based on this scale, however, but on seven tones chosen from the twelve chromatic ones, arranged in the following order: two whole tones followed by a half tone, plus three whole tones followed by a half tone. If you want to know what it sounds like, just sing the do-re-mi-fa-sol-la-ti-do that you were taught in school. (You may have forgotten it, but when you sang mi to fa, and ti to do, you were singing half tones.)

This arrangement of seven tones is called the diatonic scale in the major mode. Since there are twelve semitones within the octave span, on each of which the same seven-toned scale may be formed, there are, of course, twelve different, but similarly constructed, diatonic scales in the major mode. There are twelve

Melody

more in the minor mode, making twenty-four in all. (Further mention of the minor mode is purposely omitted in the following exposition for the sake of greater clarity.)

As an easy reference method, let us call the seven tones of the scale 1, 2, 3, 4, 5, 6, 7, without regard to whether the distance between them is a whole or half tone. As already stated, this scale may be formed on one of twelve different notes. The key to the position of the scale is found by observing the position of tone 1. If tone 1 is on the note B, then the scale is said to be in the key of B (major or minor according to the mode); if on C, C major or minor. Modulation takes place when we move from one key to another. Thus we may modulate from the key of B major to the key of C major, and vice versa.

The seven degrees of the scale also have definite relationships among themselves. They are ruled over by the first degree, tone 1, known as the tonic. At least, in pre-twentieth-century music, all melodies tend to center around the tonic. Despite heroic efforts to break the hegemony of the tonic, it is still, though not so obviously as in former times, the central point around which other notes tend to gather.

Next in power of attraction is the fifth degree, or dominant, as it is called; followed in importance by the fourth degree, or subdominant. The seventh degree is named the leading tone because it always tends to lead to the tonic. Here, again, these seemingly arbitrary relationships are all confirmed by vibrational data.

Let us summarize the scale system as explained thus far, before examining its later evolution.

Octave span:

Chromatic scale:

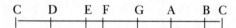

Diatonic scale:

Up to recent times, all Occidental melodies were written within this scale system. It bespeaks an amazing ingenuity on the part of composers that they should have been capable of so wide a variety of melodic invention within the narrow limits of the seven-toned diatonic scale. Here follow a few typical examples of melodies from different musical periods.

For purity of line and feeling one can hardly do better than quote from Palestrina's choral works. Part of the unworldly quality of many of Palestrina's melodies is due

Melody

to the fact that they move conjunctly, that is, stepwise from note to note, with a minimum number of skips. This restraining discipline, which makes so many of Palestrina's melodies seem smooth and imperturbable, has the added advantage of making them easy to sing. Note that in this beautiful melody from a motet for women's voices *Ave regina coelorum*, there is only one skip of a third.

The fugue subject from Bach's E flat minor *Fugue (Well Tempered Clavichord,* Book 1) is a remarkable example of a completely rounded thought in a single, short musical phrase. To analyze why this theme, consisting of only a few notes, should be so expressive is impossible. Structurally it is based on the three essential notes of the scale-tones 1, 5, and 4; E flat, B flat, and A flat. Something in the way the theme rises bravely from 1 to 5 and then, after turning about tone 5, rises again from 1 to 4, only to fall back slowly on 1—something also about the shortened rhythmic sense of the second part of the phrase—creates an extraordinary feeling of quiet but profound resignation.

What to Listen for in Music

Another example, too long for quotation here, of an entirely different type of melody in Bach is the long lined instrumental phrase to be found in the slow movement of the *Italian Concerto*. It is archetypical of a kind of florid melody, which Bach himself treated many times and with consummate mastery. Over a regularly recurring bass, the melody takes flight; built on large and generous lines, its beauty is one of proportion rather than detail.

An admirable example of pure melodic invention, which has been quoted many times, is the second theme from the first movement of Schubert's *"Unfinished" Symphony*. The "rules" of melodic construction will be of no help to anyone in analyzing this phrase. It has a curious way of seeming to fall back upon itself (or, more exactly, the G and the D), which is all the more noticeable because of the momentary reaching for a higher interval in the sixth measure. Despite its great simplicity, it makes a unique impression, reminding us of no other theme in musical literature.

I cannot resist quoting from memory a little-known

Melody

Mexican-Indian folk tune, used by Carlos Chávez in his *Sinfónia India*. It uses repeated notes and unconventional intervals, with entirely refreshing effect.

Since the beginning of the present century, composers have considerably broadened their conception of what constitutes a good melody. Richard Strauss, continuing along Wagnerian lines, produced a freer and more sinuous melodic line, of daring leaps and generally broader scope. Debussy created his music out of a much more elusive and fragmentary melodic material. Stravinsky's melodies, taken by themselves, are comparatively unimportant. They are in the manner of Russian folk song in the earlier works and patterned after classical and romantic models in the later ones.

[57]

What to Listen for in Music

The real melodic experimenters of the century were Arnold Schoenberg and his pupils. They are the only contemporaries who write melodies that have no tonal center of any kind. Instead, they choose the twelve tones of the chromatic scale, giving equal rights to each one of the semitones. Self-imposed rules forbid the repetition of any one of the twelve tones until the other eleven notes have been sounded. This larger tone gamut, plus an increased use of wider and wider skips between single notes, has left many listeners confused, if not exasperated. Schoenberg's melodies prove that the farther from the ordinary norm we go the more willingness there must be to make a conscious effort toward assimilation of the new and unfamiliar.

The American composer Roy Harris writes melodies within a middle ground. Although they are more than likely to move through all tones of the chromatic scale, they almost always turn about one central tone, giving his music a more normal tonal feeling. He possesses a fine, robust melodic gift. Here is an example of the cello melody from the conclusion of the slow movement of his *Trio* for violin, cello, and piano:*

*Reprinted from *New Music* (Vol. 9, No. 3, April, 1936), quarterly publication of the New Music Society of California. Used by permission of Roy Harris.

Melody

mp molto cantando espr.

The reader probably realizes by now that, along with composers, he must broaden his ideas as to what a melody may be. He must not expect the same kind of melody from all composers. Palestrina's melodies are more closely patterned after known models of his own time than those of Carl Maria von Weber's, for instance. It would be foolish to expect a similar melodic inspiration from both men.

Moreover, composers are far from equally gifted as melodists. Nor should their music be valued solely according to the richness of their melodic gifts. Serge Prokofieff works a seemingly inexhaustible melodic mine as compared with Stravinsky's, yet few would claim him to be the more profound musical creator.

What to Listen for in Music

Whatever the quality of the melodic line considered alone, the listener must never lose sight of its function in a composition. It should be followed like a continuous thread which leads the listener through a piece from the very beginning to the very end. Always remember that in listening to a piece of music you must hang on to the melodic line. It may disappear momentarily, withdrawn by the composer, in order to make its presence more powerfully felt when it reappears. But reappear it surely will, for it is impossible, except by rarest exception, to imagine a music, old or new, conservative or modern, without melody.

Most melodies are accompanied by more or less elaborate material of secondary interest. Don't allow the melody to become submerged by that accompanying material. Separate it in your mind from everything which surrounds it. You must be able to hear it. It is up to composer and interpreter to help you hear it that way.

As for the ability to recognize a beautiful melody when you hear one or distinguishing between a banal and a freshly inspired line, only increased experience as listener—plus the assimilation of hundreds of melodies of all kinds—can accomplish that for you.

6

The Four Elements of Music

III · HARMONY

B<small>Y COMPARISON</small> with rhythm and melody, harmony is the most sophisticated of the three musical elements. We are so accustomed to thinking of music in terms of harmonic music that we are likely to forget how recent an innovation it is, by comparison with the other elements. Rhythm and melody came naturally to man, but harmony gradually evolved from what was partly an intellectual conception—no doubt one of the most original conceptions of the human mind.

Harmony, in the sense that we think of it, was quite unknown in music until about the ninth century. Up until that time, all music of which we have any record consisted of a single melodic line. Among Oriental peoples of today, this is still true, although their single melodies are often combined with complex percussion rhythms. The anonymous composers who first began experimenting with harmonic effects were destined to change all music that came after them, at least among Occidental nations. No wonder we look upon the development of the harmonic sense as one of the most remarkable phenomena of musical history.

The birth of harmony is generally placed in the ninth century, because it is first mentioned in treatises of that period. As might be expected, the early forms of harmony sound crudely primitive to our ears. There are three principal kinds of early harmonic writing. The earliest form was called "organum." It is very easy to understand, for whenever we "harmonize" in intervals of thirds or sixths above or below a melody, we produce a kind of organum. The idea in ancient organum was the same, except that the harmonizing was done in intervals of the fourth below or fifth above, thirds and sixths being proscribed. So that

Harmony

organum is simply a single melody, plus that same melody repeated simultaneously at the fourth or fifth interval below or above, respectively. As a method of harmonization it makes a fairly primitive beginning, particularly if you imagine all music being treated in only that way. Here follows an illustration of organum:

The second of these early forms was not developed until another two or three hundred years had passed. It was called "descant" and is attributed to the ingenuity of French composers. In descant, there was no longer merely a single melody moving in parallel motion with itself but two independent melodies, moving in opposite directions. At that time, one of the basic principles of good voice leading was uncovered: When the upper voice moves downward, the lower voice moves upward; and vice versa. This innovation was doubly ingenious, for no intervals between voices, other than the originally permitted fifths, fourths, and octaves of organum, were used. In other words, they kept

[63]

the rules as to intervals but applied them in a better way. (For the benefit of those who do not know what an "interval" is, the term indicates the distance between two notes. Thus, from the note C to G there are five tones, C-D-E-F-G. C to G is therefore referred to as an interval of the fifth.) Here is an example of descant:

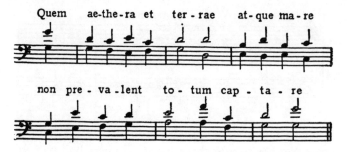

The last form of earliest counterpoint was called "faux-bourdon" (false bass). This introduced the hitherto forbidden intervals of the third and sixth, which were to form the basis of all later harmonic developments. As long as harmonic intervals were confined to fourths and fifths, the effect remained bare and crude-sounding. That is why the introduction of the more mellifluous thirds and sixths added immeasurably to harmonic resource. Credit for this step is given the English, who are said to have "harmonized in thirds" in their popular singing long before faux-bourdon made

Harmony

its more formal entry into art music. Here is an example of a melody harmonized according to faux-bourdon:

It is not my purpose to plot out a historical survey of harmonic development but only to indicate the tentative beginnings of harmony and to stress its continually evolving nature. Without understanding harmony as a gradual growth and change from primitive beginnings, the reader cannot expect to grasp the implications of harmonic innovation in the twentieth century.

The sounding together of separate tones produces chords. Harmony, considered as a science, is the study of these chords and their relationship among one another. It takes more than a year for the music student to make a comprehensive study of the underlying principles of harmonic science. Needless to say, the lay listener can expect to get only the merest smattering of information from a short chapter of this kind. Still, without cluttering the reader's mind with details, some attempt must be made to relate the harmonic element to the rest of music. To do that, the reader should have some conception, no matter how slight, of how chords are built and what their interrelations are; of the meaning of tonality and modulation; of the importance of the basic harmonic skeleton in the structure of the whole; of the relative significance of consonance and dissonance; and, finally, of the comparatively recent breakdown of the entire harmonic system as it was known in the nineteenth century and some still more recent attempts at reintegration.

Harmonic theory is based on the assumption that all chords are built from the lowest note upward in a series of intervals of a third. For example, take the note A as the bottom tone, or root, of a chord to be constructed. We are able, by building series of thirds on this root, to get the chord A-C-E-G-B-D-F. If we continued, we should simply be repeating notes that are already included in the chord. If, instead of taking the note A, we take the numeral 1 to symbolize any root, we get the following picture of any series of thirds: 1–3–5–7–9–11–13.

Theoretically, this seven-toned chord 1–3–5–7–9–11–13 is possible, but practically most of the music we know is based on only 1–3–5, which is the ordinary three-toned chord known as the triad. (A full chord is always made up of three tones or more; two-toned "chords" are too ambiguous to be counted as anything

[66]

more than intervals.) Besides the triad, the other chords
are named as follows:

			13
		11	11
	9	9	9
7	7	7	7
5	5	5	5
3	3	3	3
1	1	1	1
seventh chord	ninth chord	eleventh chord	thirteenth chord

These four chords only gradually fought their way
into the musical sun, and, each time, a minor revolution had to take place before they were admitted.
Since it is the triad 1–3–5 that accounts for most of
familiar music, let us concentrate attention on that.
If you wish to know how a triad sounds, sing "do-
mi-sol." Now sing "do-mi-sol-do," with the second
"do" an octave higher than the first one. That is still
a triad, though there are four tones in the chord. In
other words, nothing is changed, as far as theory
goes, by doubling any tone in any chord any number
of times. As a matter of fact, most of our harmonic
writing is done in four-part harmony, with one tone
doubled.

Furthermore, chords need not remain in their root
position, that is, with tone 1 as the bottom note of the
chord. For example, 1–3–5 might be inverted so as to

have 3 or 5 as the bass note of the triad. In that case, the chord would look like this:

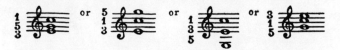

The same is true of the other chords mentioned above. The reader can already appreciate that with the possibilities of doublings and inversions, not to mention all kinds of alterations too complicated to go into here, the basic chords, though few in number, are open to wide possibilities of variation.

So far, we have been considering chords in the abstract. Now let us pin them down—always confining ourselves to the triad for simplicity's sake—to the seven tones of one specific scale. By taking the scale, for instance, of C major and building a 1–3–5 chord on each of the degrees of the scale, we get our first series of chords, which are related both to each other and to similar chords in other tonalities than that of C major. This is the moment to review what was said about scale in the previous chapter. For anything that was stated as true about the seven tones of the diatonic scale will hold true of chords constructed on those seven tones. In other words, *it is the root of the chord that is the determining factor*. Chords built on the tonic, dominant, and subdominant degrees bear the same relative attraction

Harmony

to one another as the tonic, dominant, and subdominant tones taken alone. In the same way, it is sufficient to find the tonic chord in order to determine the
tonality of a series of chords; and chords, like single
tones, are said to modulate when they move out of one
key into another.

Insomuch as they are chords and not single tones,
they do have one further connection. If we construct a
triad on the first three degrees of the scale, we get:

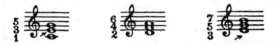

This shows that the first and third chords have tones
3 and 5 in common. This factor, that chords of the
same or different tonalities possess common tones, is
one reason for the strong feeling we have of the relationship of chords among themselves.

This brief summary of the construction of chords
and their interrelationships must suffice. Now let us
see how these harmonic facts are applied.

Just as a skyscraper has a steel frame below the outer
covering of stone and brick, so every well-made piece
of music has a solid framework underlying the outer
appearance of the musical materials. To extract and analyze that implied harmonic skeleton is the work of a
technician, but the sensitive listener will undoubtedly

know when there is something harmonically lacking, even though he may not be able to give the reason for it. The reader, perhaps, will be interested to see how, in one tiny example, the harmonic frame of a few bars of music is abstracted. Take, for instance, the first four measures of *Ach! du lieber Augustin.*

There are, in these four measures, only two underlying chords I and V, the tonic and dominant. Of course, the basic chords are not so plainly there as they would be in a harmony exercise. Music would be dull indeed if composers were not able to disguise, vary, and adorn the bare harmonic frame.

You should realize, however, that composers apply this same principle not for four measures only but for four movements of a symphony. That may give you some inkling of the problem involved. In the early days, the harmonic progressions of a piece were fairly well established in advance, by virtue of common prac-

Harmony

tice. But long after the conventions were abandoned, the principle was retained, for whatever the harmonic style of the music may be, the underlying chordal structure must have its own logic. Without it, a work is likely to lack a sense of movement. A well-knit harmonic framework will be neither too static nor over elaborate; it provides a steady foundation which is always firmly there no matter what the decorative complexities may be.

The harmonic principles outlined above are, of course, a greatly simplified version of harmonic facts as they existed up to the end of the last century. The breakup of the old system, which occurred around 1900, was no sudden decision on the part of certain revolutionaries in music. The entire history of harmonic development shows us a continually changing picture; very slowly, but inevitably, our ears are enabled to assimilate chords of greater complexity and modulations to farther off keys. Almost every epoch has its harmonic pioneers: Claudio Monteverdi and Gesualdo in the seventeenth century introduced chords that shocked their contemporaries in much the same way that Moussorgsky and Wagner shocked theirs. Still, they all had this in common: Their new chords and modulations were arrived at through a broader conception of the same harmonic theory. The reason our own period has been so remarkable in harmonic experimentation is that the entire former theory of harmony was thrown overboard, for a time at least. It was no longer a question of broadening an old system but of creating something entirely new.

The line of demarcation comes soon after Wagner. Debussy, Schoenberg, and Stravinsky were the main pathfinders in this uncharted harmonic territory. Wagner had begun the destruction of the older harmonic language because of his chromaticism. I have already explained that our system, as practiced without question up to the end of the nineteenth century, admitted the hegemony of one main tonic note in the scale and, therefore, one main tonality in a piece of music. Modulation to other tonalities were looked upon as only temporary. Inevitably, a return to the tonic key was implied. Since there are twelve different diatonic scales, modulation may be represented by the face of a clock, with XII symbolizing the tonic key. Seventeenth- and eighteenth-century composers did not venture far in their modulatory schemes. They would go from XII to I to XI and back to XII. Later composers were bolder, but the return to XII was still imperative. Wagner, however, moved about from one tonality to another to such an extent that the feeling of a central key or tonality began to be lost. He modulated daringly from XII to VI to IX to III, etc., and one could not be sure when, if ever, the return to the central to-nality would be made.

Schoenberg drew the logical conclusions of this harmonic ambiguity, abandoning the principle of tonality altogether. His type of harmony is generally referred to as "atonality," to distinguish it from music of tonality.* What was left was the series of twelve "equal" semitones of the chromatic scale. Schoenberg himself found this remainder somewhat anarchical in later years and began the construction of a new system for handling these twelve equal semitones which he named the twelve-tone system. I shall do no more than mention it, for an adequate explanation would take us too far afield.

Debussy, though less radical harmonically than Schoenberg, preceded him in starting the breakdown of the old system. Debussy, one of the most instinctive musicians who ever lived, was the first composer of our time who dared to make his ear the sole judge of what was good harmonically. With Debussy, analysts found chords that could no longer be explained according to the old harmony. If one had asked Debussy why he used such chords, I am sure he would have given the only possible answer: "I like it that way!" It is as if one composer finally had confidence

---

*Schoenberg did not approve of the term "atonality." The word continues to be used nonetheless, more out of convenience than because of its exactitude.

in his ear. I exaggerate a little, for, after all, composers have never had to wait for theoreticians to tell them what or what not to do. On the contrary, it has always been the other way about—theoreticians have explained the logic of the composer's thought after he has instinctively put it down.

At any rate, what Debussy accomplished was the sweeping aside of all previously held theories of harmonic science. His work inaugurated a period of complete harmonic freedom, which has been a stumbling block for innumerable listeners ever since. They complain that this new music is full of "dissonances" and that all past musical history proves that there must always be a sensible mixture of consonance and dissonance.

This question of consonance and dissonance deserves a paragraph to itself, if we are to remove the stumbling block. The whole problem, as has been pointed out many times, is a purely relative one. To say that a consonance is a pleasant-sounding chord, and a dissonance unpleasant, is making the case much too simple. For a chord is more or less dissonant to you according to the period in which you live, according to your listening experience, and according to whether the chord is played fortissimo in the brass instruments or caressed pianissimo in the strings. So that a dissonance is only relative—relative to you, your epoch, and the place that it holds in the piece as a whole. This does not deny the existence of dissonance, as some commentators seem to do, but merely that the proper mixture of consonance and dissonance is a matter to be left to the composer's discretion. If all new music sounds continually and unrelievedly dissonant to you, then it is a safe guess that your listening experience is insufficient as regards music of your own time—which is not so strange in the majority of cases, when we realize the small proportion of new music heard by the average listener compared with what he hears of the music of former times.

One other important harmonic innovation was introduced before World War I. At first, it was confused with atonality because of its similarly revolutionary sound. But actually, it was the exact opposite of atonality, in that it reaffirmed the principle of tonality and reaffirmed it doubly. That is to say, not content with one tonality, it introduced the idea of sounding two or more separate tonalities simultaneously. This process, which Darius Milhaud has used most effectively at times, became known as "polytonality." A clear example of it is to be found in *Corcovado*, one of Milhaud's pieces on Brazilian themes, *Saudades do Brazil*, in which the right hand plays in the key of D major while the left hand essays G major. Here, again, if you are inclined to be disturbed by the polytonalities of new music, one can only advise you to listen until they become as familiar to you as the music of Schumann or Chopin. If you do that, you may not find the music any the more to your liking (for, needless to add, not all polytonal music is good music), but it will no longer be the "dissonances" produced by the clash of harmonies that disturb you.

The harmonic revolution of the first half of the twentieth century is now definitely at an end. Polytonality and atonality have both become a normal part of current musical usage. One unexpected development should be noted: the recrudescence of interest, at the end of World War II, in the twelve-tone method of Arnold Schoenberg, especially in countries like Italy, France, and Switzerland, where there had previously been little or no sign of influence. Composers like the Italian Luigi Dallapiccola or the Swiss Frank Martin have not hesitated to extract tonal implications from the dodecaphonic (twelve-tone) method, thereby removing some of its panchromatic sting. Younger composers, adherents of Schoenberg's more radical pupil Anton Webern, have persisted in writing a music more rigorously athematic and atonal than that of the Viennese master himself.

Harmony

Despite harmonic innovations, a large part of contemporary music remains basically diatonic and tonal. But it is no longer the diatonic, tonal harmony of the period before the turn of the century. Like most revolutions, this one has left its mark on our harmonic language. As a result, music written nowadays may often be said to be tonally centered even though it may have no tonality analyzable in the old sense. This tendency toward harmonic conservatism is certain to help bridge the gap between the contemporary composer and his audience. With the familiarity bred of phonograph disk, radio, and film track the daring harmonies of the day before yesterday are gradually and painlessly being assimilated into the musical language of our time.

7

The Four Elements of Music

IV • TONE COLOR

AFTER rhythm, melody, and harmony, comes timbre, or tone color. Just as it is impossible to hear speech without hearing some specific timbre, so music can exist only in terms of some specific color in tone. Timbre in music is analogous to color in painting. It is a fascinating element, not only because of vast resources already explored but also because of illimitable future possibilities.

[78]

Tone Color

Tone color in music is that quality of sound produced by a particular medium of musical tone production. That is a formal definition of something which is perfectly familiar to everyone. Just as most mortals know the difference between white and green, so the recognition of differences in tone color is an innate sense with which most of us are born. It is difficult to imagine a person so "tone-blind" that he cannot tell a bass voice from a soprano or, to put it instrumentally, a tuba from a cello. It is not a question of knowing the names of the voices or instruments but simply of recognizing the difference in their tone quality, if both were heard from behind a screen.

Instinctively, therefore, everyone has a good start toward getting a fuller understanding of the various aspects of tone color. Don't allow this natural appreciation to limit your taste for certain favorite tone colors to the exclusion of all others. I am thinking of the man who adores the sound of a violin but feels an extreme distaste for any other instrument. The experienced listener should wish rather to broaden his appreciation to include every known species of tone color. Moreover, although I have said that every person can make broad distinctions in tone colors, there are also subtle differences that only experience in listening can clear up. Even a music student, in the beginning, has difficulty in distinguishing the tone of a clarinet from that of its blood brother the bass clarinet.

The intelligent listener should have two main objectives in relation to tone color: (*a*) to sharpen his awareness of different instruments and their separate tonal characteristics and (*b*) to gain a better appreciation of the composer's expressive purpose in using any instrument or combination of instruments.

Before exploring the separate instruments for their individual tone qualities, the attitude of the composer toward his instrumental possibilities should be more fully explained. After all, not every musical theme is born fully swaddled in a tonal dress. Very often the composer finds himself with a theme that can be equally well played on the violin, flute, clarinet, trumpet, or half a dozen other instruments. What, then, makes him decide to choose one rather than another? Only one thing: he chooses the instrument with the tone color that best expresses the meaning behind his idea. In other words, his choice is determined by the expressive value of any specific instrument. That is true in the case not only of single instruments but also of combinations of instruments. The composer who chooses a bassoon rather than an oboe in certain instances may also have to decide whether his musical idea best belongs in a string ensemble or a full orchestra. And the thing that makes him decide in every case will be the expressive meaning that he wishes to convey.

At times, of course, a composer conceives a theme and its tonal investiture instantaneously. There are outstanding examples of that in music. One that is often quoted is the flute solo at the beginning of *L'après midi d'un faune (Afternoon of a Faun)*. That same theme, played by any other instrument than the flute, would induce a very different emotional feeling. It is impossible to imagine Debussy's conceiving the theme first and then later deciding to orchestrate it for a flute. The two must have been conceived simultaneously. But that does not settle the matter.

For even in the case of themes that come to the composer in their full orchestral panoply, later musical developments in the course of a particular piece may bring on the need for varied orchestral treatments of the same theme. In such a case, the composer is like a playwright deciding on a dress for an actress in a particular scene. The stage shows us an actress seated on a bench in a park. The playwright may wish to have her clothed in such a way that the spectator knows as soon as the curtain rises what mood she is in. It is not just a pretty dress; it's an especially designed dress to give you a particular feeling about this particular character in this particular scene. The same holds true for the composer who "dresses" a musical theme. The entire gamut of tonal color at his disposal is so rich that nothing but a clear conception of the emotional feeling that he wishes to convey can make him decide as between one instrument and another or one group of instruments and another.

The idea of the inevitable connection of a specific color for a specific music is a comparatively modern one. It seems likely that composers before Handel's time did not have a strong feeling for instrumental color. At any rate, most of them did not even trouble to write down explicitly what instrument was desired for a particular part. Apparently it was a matter of indifference to them whether a four-part score was executed by four wood-wind instruments or four strings. Nowadays composers insist on certain instruments for certain ideas, and they have come to write for them in a way so characteristic that a violin part may be unplayable on an oboe even when they are confined to the same register.

Each of the separate tone colors that the composer is enabled to use only gradually found its way into music. Three steps were generally involved. First, the instrument had to be invented. Since instruments, like any other invention, usually begin in some primitive form, the second step was the perfecting of the instrument. Thirdly, players had gradually to achieve technical mastery of the new instrument. That is the story of the piano, the violin, and most other instruments.

Of course, every instrument, no matter how perfected, has its limitations. There are limitations of range, of dynamics, of execution. Each instrument can play so low and no lower, so high and no higher. A composer may wish at times that the oboe could play just half a tone lower than it does. But there is no help for it; these limits are prescribed. So are dynamic limitations. A trumpet, though it plays loudly by comparison with a violin, cannot play more loudly than it can. Composers are sometimes painfully aware of that fact, but there is no getting around it.

Difficulties of execution must also be continually borne in mind by the composer. A melodic idea that seems predestined to be sung by a clarinet will be found to make use of a particular group of notes that present insuperable difficulties to the clarinetist because of certain constructional peculiarities of his instrument. These same notes may be quite easy to perform on oboe or bassoon, but it so happens that on a clarinet they are very difficult. So composers are not completely free agents in making their choice of tone colors.

[83]

Nevertheless they are in a much better position than were their predecessors. Just because instruments are machines, subject to improvement like any other machine, any contemporary composer enjoys advantages that Beethoven did not have as far as mere tone color is concerned. The present-day composer has new and improved materials to work with, besides which he benefits from the experience of his forebears. This is especially true of his use of the orchestra. No wonder that critics who pride themselves on their severity toward contemporary music willingly allow the brilliance and cleverness of the modern composer's handling of the orchestra.

It is important nowadays for a composer to have a feeling for the essential nature of each instrument—how it may best be used to exploit its most personal characteristics. I should like to take, for example, a perfectly familiar instrument—the piano—and show what I mean by using an instrument characteristically. A treatise on orchestration would do the same for each of the instruments.

The piano is a handy instrument to have around—"maid of all work," someone once called it. It can substitute for a large variety of different instruments including the orchestra itself. But it is also a being in its own right—it is also a piano—and as such it has

Tone Color

properties and characteristics that belong to itself alone. The composer who exploits the piano for its essential nature will be using it to best advantage. Let us see what that essential nature is.

A piano may be used in one of two ways: either as a vibrating or as a nonvibrating instrument. That is true because of its construction, which consists of series of strings stretched across a steel frame, with a damper on each string. This damper is vital to the nature of the instrument. It is controlled by the piano pedal. When the pedal is untouched, piano tone lasts only as long as the note is pressed by the pianist's finger. But if the damper is removed (by pushing the pedal down), the tone is sustained. In either case, piano tone declines in intensity from the instant it is struck. The pedal minimizes this weakness somewhat and therefore holds the key to good piano writing.

Although the piano was invented around 1711 by one Cristofori, it was not until the middle nineteenth century that composers understood how to take advantage of the pedal in a truly characteristic way. Chopin, Schumann, and Liszt were masters of piano writing because they took fully into account its peculiarities as a vibrating instrument. Debussy and Ravel in France, Scriabin in Russia carried on the tradition of Chopin and Liszt, as far as their piano writing is concerned.

All of them took full cognizance of the fact that the piano is, on one side of its nature, a collection of sympathetically vibrating strings, producing a sensuous and velvety or brilliant and brittle conglomeration of tones, which are capable of immediate extinction through release of the damper pedal.

More recent composers have exploited the other side of the piano's essential nature—the nonvibrating tone.

The nonvibrating piano is the piano in which little or no use is made of the pedal. Played thus, a hard, dry piano tone is produced which has its own particular virtue. The feeling of the modern composer for harsh, percussive tonal effects found valuable outlet in this new use of the piano, turning it into a kind of large xylophone. Excellent examples of this may be found in the piano works of such moderns as Bela Bartók, Carlos Chávez or Arthur Honegger. This last composer has an attractive last movement in his *Concertino* for piano and orchestra which fairly crackles with a dry, brittle piano sonority.

The point I have been making in relation to the piano is valid for every other instrument also. There is definitely a characteristic way of writing for each one of them. The tonal colors that an instrument can produce that are uniquely its own are the ones sought after by the composer.

Tone Color

SINGLE TONE COLORS

Now we are in a better position to examine single tone colors, such as are found in the usual symphony orchestra. Orchestral instruments are generally taken as a norm, for it is those that we are most apt to find in a composer's score. Later we shall want to know how these single tone colors are mixed to form timbres of various instrumental combinations.

Orchestral instruments are divided into four principal types, or sections. The first section, of course, is that of the strings; the second, of the woodwind; the third is the brass; and the fourth is the percussion. Each of these sections is made up of a related group of instruments of similar type. Every composer, when working, keeps these four divisions very much to the front of his mind.

The string section, which is the most used of all, is itself made up of four different types of stringed instruments. These are the violin, the viola, the violoncello (or cello, for short), and the double bass.

The instrument with which you are most familiar is, of course, the violin. In orchestral writing, violins are divided into two sections—so-called first and second violins—but only one type of instrument is involved. There is certainly no need to describe the lyric, singing quality of the violin; it is much too familiar to all of us. But you may be less familiar with certain special effects which help to give the instrument a greater variety of tone color.

Most important of these is the pizzicato, in which the string is plucked by the finger instead of being played with the bow, thus producing a somewhat guitar-like effect. That, too, is familiar enough to most of us. Less well-known is the effect of harmonics, as they are called. These are produced by not pressing the finger on the string in the usual way but lightly touching it instead, thereby creating a flute-like tone of special charm. Double stopping means playing on two or more strings simultaneously, so that a chordal effect is obtained. Finally, there is the veiled and sensitive tone obtainable through use of the mute, a small extra contraption placed on the bridge of the instrument, immediately deadening the sonority.

All of these varied effects are obtainable not only on the violin but also on all the other stringed instruments.

The viola is an instrument that is often confused with the violin, because it not only resembles it in outward appearance but is held and played in the same fashion. Closer examination would show that it is a slightly larger and weightier instrument, producing a heavier and graver tone. It cannot sing notes as high as the violin's but compensates for that by being able to sing lower. It plays a contralto role to the violin's soprano. If it lacks the light lyric quality of the higher instrument, it possesses, on the other hand, a gravely expressive sonority—seemingly full of emotion.

The cello is a more easily recognized instrument played, as it is, by a seated performer holding it firmly propped between both knees. It plays baritone and bass to the viola's contralto. Its range is one full octave lower than the viola, but it pays for this by not being able to go so high. The quality of cello tone is well known. Composers, however, are conscious of three different registers. In its upper register, the cello can be a very poignant and touching instrument. At the other extreme of its range, the sonority is one of sober profundity. The middle register, most frequently used, produces the more familiar cello tone—a serious, smooth, baritone-like quality of sound, almost always expressive of some degree of feeling.

The last of the string family, the double bass, is the largest of all and must be played standing. Because it is seen in jazz bands, it has recently taken on an importance more nearly commensurate with its size. When it was first used in orchestras, it played a very menial role, doing little more than what the cello did (doubling the bass, as it is called) an octave lower. This it does very well. Later composers gave it a part of its own to play, down in the depths of the orchestra. It almost never functions as a solo instrument; and if you have ever heard a double bass try to sing a melody, you will understand why. The proper function of the double bass is to supply a firm foundation for the entire structure above it.

The second section of orchestral instruments comprises those that come under the heading of woodwinds. Once again they are of four different types, though in this case each type has a closely related instrument which belongs in its immediate group, a kind of first cousin to the main type. The four principal woodwinds are the flute, oboe, clarinet, and bassoon. The flute's "first cousins" are the piccolo and the flute in G; the oboe is related to the English horn, which, as one orchestration book has it, is neither English nor a horn but called that nevertheless. The clarinet is related to the clarinet piccolo and bass clarinet; and the bassoon, to the double bassoon.

Recently a new instrument has been added, which is partly a woodwind, called the saxophone. You've probably heard of it! At first, it was only very sparingly used in the usual symphonic orchestra. Then suddenly the jazz band began exploiting it, and now it is finding its way back to more extended use in the symphonic field.

Even if all the instruments of the orchestra are playing their loudest, you can generally hear the piccolo above all of them. In fortissimo, it possesses a thin but shrill and brilliant sonority and can outpipe anyone within listening distance. Composers are careful how they use it. Often it merely doubles, an octave higher, what the flute is doing. But recent composers have shown that, played quietly in its more moderate register, it has a thin singing voice of no little charm.

The tone color of the flute is fairly well known. It possesses a soft, cool, fluid or feathery timbre. Because of its very defined personality, it is one of the most attractive instruments in the orchestra. It is extremely agile; it can play faster and more notes to the second than any other member of the woodwinds. Most listeners are familiar with its upper register. Much use has been made in recent years of its lowest register which is darkly expressive, in a most individual way.

The oboe is a nasal-sounding instrument, quite different in tone quality from the flute. (The oboe player holds his instrument perpendicularly, whereas the flutist holds his horizontally.) The oboe is the most expressive of the woodwinds, expressive in a very subjective way. By comparison, the flute seems impersonal. The oboe has a certain pastoral quality which is often put to good use by composers. More than any other woodwind the oboe must be well played if its limited tonal scope is to be sufficiently varied.

The English horn is a kind of baritone oboe, which is often, by inexperienced listeners, confused in tone color with the oboe. It possesses a plaintive quality all its own, however, which was fully exploited by Wagner in the introduction to the third act of *Tristan and Isolde.*

The clarinet has a smooth, open, almost hollow sound. It is a cooler, more even-sounding instrument than the oboe, being also more brilliant. Much closer to the flute than to the oboe in quality, it has almost as great an agility as the former, singing with an equal grace melodies of all kinds. In its lowest octave it possesses a unique tone color of a deeply haunting effect. Its dynamic range is more remarkable than that of any other woodwind, extending from a mere whisper to the most brilliant fortissimo.

The bass clarinet hardly differs from the clarinet itself, except that its range is one octave lower. In its bottom register, it has a ghostlike quality which is not easily forgotten.

The bassoon is one of the most versatile of instruments. It is able to do a number of different things. In its upper register, it has a plaintive sound which is very special. Stravinsky made excellent use of that timbre at the very beginning of the *Sacre du Printemps (Rites of Spring)*. On the other hand, the bassoon produces a dry, humorous staccato in the lower register, of an almost puckish effect. And it is always being called upon to make dullish bass parts more resonant by the sheer weight of its tone. A handy instrument it certainly is.

The double bassoon bears the same relationship to it as the double bass does to the cello. Ravel used it to characterize the beast in his *Beauty and the Beast* from the *Mother Goose Suite*. Mainly it helps to supply a bass voice to the orchestra where it is badly needed, down in its very depths.

The brass section, like the others, boasts four principal types of instruments. These are the horn (or French horn, to be exact), the trumpet, the trombone, and the tuba. (The cornet is too much like the trumpet to need special mention.)

The French horn is an instrument with a lovely round tone—a soft, satisfying, almost liquid tone. Played loud, it takes on a majestic, brassy quality which is the complete opposite of its softer tone. If there exists a more noble sound than eight horns singing a melody fortissimo in unison, I have never heard it. There is one other most effective sonority to be obtained from the horn by stopping the tone either with a mute or with the hand placed in the bell of the instrument. A choked, rasping sound is produced when the tone is forced. The same procedure, when unforced, gives an unearthly tone which seems to emanate with magical effect from distant places.

The trumpet is that brilliant, sharp, commanding instrument with which everyone is familiar. It is the mainstay of all composers at climactic moments. But it also possesses a beautiful tone when played softly. Like the horn it has its special mutes, which produce a snarling, strident sonority which is indispensable in dramatic moments and a soft, dulcet, flutelike voice when played *piano*. Recently, jazz-band trumpetists have made use of a large assortment of mutes, each producing a quite different sonority. Eventually some of these are almost certain to be introduced into the symphony orchestra.

The tone of the trombone is allied in quality to that of the French horn. It also possesses a noble and majestic sound, one that is even larger and rounder than the horn's tone. But it also partly belongs with the trumpet, because of its brilliance of timbre in fortissimo. Moments of grandeur and solemnity are often due to a judicious use of the trombone section of the orchestra.

The tuba is one of the orchestra's more spectacular-looking instruments, since it fills the arms of the player holding it. It isn't easily manageable. To play it at all one must possess good teeth and plenty of reserve wind. It is a heavier, more dignified, harder-to-move kind of trombone. It is seldom used melodically, though in recent years composers have entrusted occasional themes to its bearlike mercies, with varying results. (Ravel's tuba solo in his orchestral version of Moussorgsky's *Pictures at an Exhibition* is a particularly happy example.) For the most part, however, its function is to emphasize the bass, and, as such, it does valuable service.

The fourth section of the orchestra is made up of various kinds of percussion instruments. Everyone who attends a concert notices this section, perhaps too much. With a few exceptions, these instruments have no definite pitch. They are generally used in one of three ways: to sharpen rhythmic effects, dynamically to heighten the sense of climax, or to add color to the other instruments. Their effectiveness is in inverse ratio to the use that is made of them. In other words, the more they are saved for essential moments the more effective they will be.

In the percussion group, it is the drum family that is most imposing. These are all rhythm- and noise-makers of various sizes and assortments, from the little tom-tom to the big bass drum. The only drum with a definite pitch is the well-known kettledrum, usually found in groups of two or three. Played with two sticks, its dynamic range goes all the way from a shadowy, far-off rumble to an overpowering succession of thudlike beats. Other noisemakers, though not of the drum variety, are the cymbals; the gong, or tam-tam; the wood block; the triangle; the slapstick; and many more.

Other percussion-group instruments provide color rather than noise or rhythm. These are likely to be of definite pitch, such as the celesta and glockenspiel, the xylophone, the vibraphone, the tubular bells, and others. The first two produce tiny, bell-like tones which are a great asset to the colorist in music. The xylophone is possibly the most familiar of this group, and the vibraphone the most recent addition. Well-known instruments like the harp, guitar, and mandolin are also sometimes grouped with the percussion instruments because of their plucked-string timbre. In recent years, the piano has been used as an integral part of the orchestra.

There are, of course, a number of nonorchestral instruments, such as the organ, the harmonium, the accordion—not to mention the human voice—which we can do little more than list. Needless to add, all these are sometimes used with orchestra.

MIXED TONE COLORS

Mixing these separate instruments in different combinations is one of the composer's more pleasant occupations. Though there are theoretically a very large number of possible combinations, composers usually confine themselves to groups of instruments that usage has made familiar. These may be groupings of instruments belonging to the same family, such as the string quartet, or those of different families, like flute, cello, and harp. It isn't possible to do more than mention a few customary combinations: trio, made up of violin, cello, and piano; the woodwind quintet, a combination of flute, oboe, clarinet, bassoon, and horn; the clarinet quintet (with strings); the flute, clarinet, and bassoon trio. In recent years, composers have done a considerable amount of experimenting in less usual combinations with varied results. One of the most original and successful is the accompanying orchestra of Stravinsky's ballet *Les Noces*, comprised of four pianos and thirteen percussion instruments.

The most usual of all chamber-music combinations

is that of the string quartet, composed of two violins, viola, and cello. If a composer is subjectively inclined, there is no better medium for him than the string quartet. Its very timbre creates a sense of intimacy and personal feeling which finds its best frame in a room where contact with the sonority of the instruments is a close one. The limits of the medium must never be lost sight of; composers are often guilty of trying to make the string quartet sound like a small orchestra. Within its own frame it is an admirably polyphonic medium, by which I mean that it exists in terms of the separate voices of the four instruments. In listening to the string quartet, you must be prepared to listen contrapuntally. What that means will become clearer later on when the chapter on musical texture is reached.

The symphony orchestra is, without doubt, the most interesting combination of instruments composers have yet evolved. It is equally fascinating from the listener's standpoint, for it contains within itself all instrumental combinations, of an endless variety.

In listening to the orchestra, it is wise to keep well in mind the four principal sections and their relative importance. Don't become hypnotized by the antics of the kettledrum player, no matter how absorbing they may be. Don't concentrate on the string section alone, just because they are seated up front nearest

Tone Color

you. Try to free yourself of bad orchestral listening habits. The main thing you can do in listening to the orchestra, aside from enjoying the sheer beauty of the sound itself, is to extricate the principal melodic material from its surrounding and supporting elements. The melodic line generally passes from one section to another or from one instrument to another, and you must always be mentally alert if you expect to be able to follow its peregrinations. The composer helps by careful balancing of his instrumental sonorities; the conductor helps by realizing those balances, adjusting individual conditions to the composer's intention. But none can be of any help if you are not prepared to disengage the melodic material from its accompanying web of sound.

The conductor, if rightly looked at, may be of some help in this. He generally will be found giving his primary attention to the instruments who have the main melody. If you watch what he is doing, you will be able to tell, without previous knowledge of a piece, where the center of your interest should be. It goes without saying that a good conductor will confine himself to necessary gestures; otherwise he can be most distracting.

A chapter on tone color, written in America, would be incomplete without some mention of the jazz band,

our own original contribution to new orchestral timbres. The jazz band is a real creation in novel tonal
effects, whether you like them or not. It is the absence
of strings and the resultant dependence on brass and
wind as melody instruments that makes the modern
dance band sound so different from a Viennese waltz
orchestra. If you listen to a jazz band closely, you will
discover that certain instruments provide the rhythmic
background (piano, banjo, bass, and percussion), others the harmonic texture, with, as a rule, one solo
instrument playing the melody. Trumpet, clarinet, saxophone, and trombone are used interchangeably as harmonic or melodic instruments. The real fun begins
when the melody is counterpointed by one or more
subsidiary ones, making for an intricacy of melodic and
rhythmic elements that only the closest listening can
unravel. There is no reason why you should not use
the jazz band as a way of practising how mentally to
disconnect separate musical elements. When the band
is at its best, it will set you problems aplenty.

8

Musical Texture

IN ORDER better to understand what to listen for in music, the layman should, in a general way, be able to distinguish three different kinds of musical texture. There are three species of texture: monophonic, homophonic, and polyphonic.

Monophonic music is, of course, the simplest of all. It is music of a single, unaccompanied melodic line. Chinese or Hindu music is monophonic in texture. No harmony, in our sense, accompanies their melodic line. The line itself, aside from a complex rhythmic percussion accompaniment, is of an extraordinary finesse and subtlety, making use of quarter tones and other smaller intervals unknown in our system. Not only all Oriental peoples but also the Greeks had a music that was monophonic in texture.

The finest development of monophony in our own music is Gregorian chant. From uncertain beginnings in very early church music, its expressive power became greatly enhanced by generations of church composers' working and reworking a similar material. It is the best example we have in Western music of an unaccompanied melodic line.

In later times, the use of monophony has usually been incidental. The music seems to pause for a moment, concentrating attention on a single line, thereby producing an effect similar to an open space in a landscape. There are, of course, examples of monophonic writing in sonatas for solo instruments, such as flute or cello, by eighteenth- and twentieth-century composers. Because of hundreds of years of accompanying harmonies, these single-lined works often suggest an implied harmony, even though none is actually sounded. In general, monophony is the clearest of all textures and presents no listening problems.

Musical Texture

The second species—homophonic texture—is only slightly more difficult to hear immediately than monophony. It is also more important for us as listeners, because of its constant use in music. It consists of a principal melodic line and a chordal accompaniment. As long as music was vocally and contrapuntally conceived—that is, until the end of the sixteenth century—homophonic texture in our sense was unknown. Homophony was the "invention" of the early Italian opera composers who sought a more direct way of imparting dramatic emotion and a clearer setting of the text than was possible through contrapuntal methods.

What happened is fairly easy to explain. There are two ways of considering a simple succession of chords. Either we may consider it contrapuntally, that is, each separate voice of one chord moving to its next note in the following chord; or we may think of it harmonically, in which case no thought of the separate voices is retained. The point is that the predecessors of the Italian innovators of the seventeenth century never thought of their harmonies except in the first way, as resulting from the combination of separate melodic voices. The revolutionary step was taken when all emphasis was placed upon a single line, and all other elements reduced to the status of mere accompanying chords.

What to Listen for in Music

Here is an early example of homophonic music from Caccini, showing the "newer," plainer kind of chordal accompaniment. It is necessary to have a fair amount of historical perspective to realize how original this seemed to its first listeners.

It wasn't very long before these simple chords were broken up, or figurated, as it is called. Nothing is essentially changed by figurating or turning these chords into flowing arpeggios. Once discovered, this device was soon elaborated and has exerted an unusual fascination on composers ever since. The foregoing example in chordal figuration would appear thus:

O cor' di don - na per al - trui soc -

cor - so, E ti gree d'or - so

The only texture in music that poses real listening problems is the third kind—polyphonic texture. Music that is polyphonically written makes greater demands on the attention of the listener, because it moves by reason of separate and independent melodic strands, which together form harmonies. The difficulty arises from the fact that our listening habits are formed by music that is harmonically conceived, and polyphonic music demands that we listen in a more linear fashion, disregarding, in a sense, those resultant harmonies.

No listener can afford to ignore this point, for it is fundamental to a more intelligent approach toward listening. We must always remember that all music written before the year 1600 and much that was written later was music of polyphonic texture, so that when you listen to music of Palestrina or Orlando di Lasso, you must listen differently from the way you listen to Schubert or Chopin. That is true not only from the standpoint of its emotional meaning but also, technically, because the music was conceived in an entirely different way. Polyphonic texture implies a listener who can hear separate strands of melody sung by separate voices, instead of hearing only the sound of all the voices as they happen from moment to moment, vertical fashion.

No point in this book needs direct musical illustration more than this one. The reader cannot expect to grasp it thoroughly without listening to the same piece of music over and over, making a mental effort to disentangle the interweaving voices. Here we must confine ourselves to a single illustration: Bach's well-known chorale prelude *Ich ruf' zu Dir, Herr Jesu Crist*.

Musical Texture

This is an example of three-voiced polyphony. As a bit of laboratory work, you should listen to this short piece four times, hearing first the part that is always easiest to hear—the top, or soprano, part. Now listen again, this time for the bass part which moves in a well-poised manner, making use of repeated notes. The alto, or middle voice, should be listened for next. This voice is a kind of figurated melody, but it is distinguishable from the others because of its sixteenth-note (faster) motion. Now hear all three voices together, keeping them well apart in your mind: the soprano with its sustained melody, the alto with the more flowing inner melody, and the bass with its poised line. A supplementary experiment might consist of hearing two voices at a time: soprano and bass, alto and soprano, bass and alto, before hearing all three voices together. (For the purposes of this investigation, RCA Victor's Stokowski arrangement is recommended.*)

In carrying out this little experiment, you will be doing a very valuable thing for yourself. Until you can hear all polyphonic music in this way—in terms of voice against voice, line against line—you will not be listening properly.

Polyphonic texture brings with it the question of

---

*Available only on 78-rpm recording.

how many independent voices the human ear can grasp simultaneously. Opinions differ as to that. Even composers have occasionally attacked polyphony, holding it to be an intellectual idea that has been forced upon us—not a natural one. Nevertheless, I think it can safely be maintained that with a fair amount of listening experience, two- or three-voiced music can be heard without too much mental strain. Real trouble begins when the polyphony consists of four, five, six, or eight separate and independent voices. But, as a rule, listening polyphonically is aided by the composer because he seldom keeps all the voices going at the same time. Even in four-voiced polyphony, composers so manage that one voice is usually silent while the other three are active. This lightens the burden considerably.

There is also this to be said for polyphonic music: that repeated hearings keep up your interest better than music of homophonic texture. Even supposing that you do not hear all the separate voices equally well, there is every likelihood that when you return to it again, there will be something different for you to listen to. You can always hear it from a different angle.

But whether one can hear several voices at a time or not is now merely an academic question, since so much

Musical Texture

of the world's great music has been written on the principle of polyphonic listening.

Moreover, contemporary composers have shown a marked leaning toward a renewal of interest in polyphonic writing. This was brought on as part of the general reaction against nineteenth-century music, which is basically homophonic in texture. Because the newer composers feel more sympathy with the esthetic ideals of the eighteenth century, they also have taken over the contrapuntal texture of that period—but with this difference: that their independent part writing results in harmonies that are no longer conventional. This newer kind of contrapuntal writing has sometimes been called linear, or "dissonant," counterpoint. From the listener's standpoint, there is less chance of losing the sense of the separateness of each voice in modern counterpoint, since there is no mellifluous harmonic web to fall back upon. In recent contrapuntal writing, the voices "stick" out, as it were; for it is their separateness rather than their togetherness which is stressed.

Here is an example of the newer counterpoint from Hindemith, who is one of the best practitioners of modern polyphonic texture:*

*From *Das Marienleben* (original version) by Paul Hindemith. Used by permission of Associated Music Publishers, Inc.

Remember, then, that music of polyphonic texture, whether it is by Bach or by Hindemith, is listened to in exactly the same way.

Not all music, of course, is divided into one of these three different kinds of texture. In any piece of music, the composer may go from one kind to another without transition. You, as listener, must be prepared to follow the species of texture that the composer chooses for any given moment. His choice is, in itself, not without emotional significance. Obviously, a single unaccompanied melodic line produces a greater sense of freedom and direct personal expression than a complicated web of sound. Homophonic music, which depends so much on harmonic background for its effect, generally has more immediate appeal for the listener than polyphonic music. But polyphonic music brings with it a greater intellectual participation. The mere fact that you must listen more actively in order to hear what goes on in itself induces a greater intellectual effort. Composers, as a rule, also put more mental effort into writing polyphonic music. By utilizing all three kinds of texture in a single piece, a greater variety of expressive feeling is obtained.

The Allegretto movement from Beethoven's *Seventh Symphony* provides as good an example as any of a varied texture in one of the masterworks of music. (Toscanini's RCA Victor recording is recommended.) The beginning is almost entirely chordal, with only a suggestion of a melodic phrase in the upper voice. In any case, it is definitely homophonic in texture. Then a new and full-sung melody is added in the violas and half the cellos. The effect is only partly contrapuntal, because the accompanying upper and lower voices are little more than a suggestive reminder of the opening chordal structure. But much later on (toward the end of the first side of the record), a purely contrapuntal section is arrived at. The first and second violins begin to weave a polyphonic texture about a fragment taken from the first rather inexpressive theme. If you are able to follow the way in which, gradually, the sixteenth-note motion engendered in this contrapuntal part is superimposed above a fortissimo sounding of the opening chords, you will be coming closer to the actual way in which Beethoven conceived the climax of the movement. Here, as always, a greater awareness in listening will be repaid by closer contact with the composer's thought—and not only in the technical sense, for a greater sensitivity to musical texture is certain to make the expressive meaning of music more completely felt.

A fuller understanding of contrapuntal texture and its relation to homophony will come, no doubt, when the reader has had the opportunity to consider the chapters on fundamental forms. Particularly the discussion of fugal forms should make the hearing of polyphonic texture easier.

9

Musical Structure

ALMOST anyone can more readily distinguish melodies and rhythms, or even harmonies, than the structural background of a lengthy piece of music. That is why our main emphasis, from here on, must be put upon structure in music; for the reader should realize that one of the principal things to listen for, when listening more consciously, is the planned design that binds an entire composition together.

What to Listen for in Music

Structure in music is no different from structure in any other art; it is simply the coherent organization of the artist's material. But the material in music is of a fluid and rather abstract character; therefore the composer's structural task is doubly difficult because of the very nature of music itself.

The general tendency, in explaining form in music, has been to oversimplify. The usual method is to seize upon certain well-known formal molds and demonstrate how composers write works within these molds, to a greater or lesser extent. Close examination of most masterworks, however, will show that they seldom fit so neatly as they are supposed to into the exteriorized forms of the textbooks. The conclusion is inescapable that it is insufficient to assume that structure in music is simply a matter of choosing a formal mold and then filling it with inspired tones. Rightly understood, form can only be the gradual growth of a living organism from whatever premise the composer starts. It follows, then, that "the form of every genuine piece of music is unique." It is musical content that determines form.

Nevertheless, composers are not by any means entirely independent of outer formal molds. It therefore becomes necessary for the listener to understand this relationship between the given, or chosen, form and the composer's independence of that form. Two things, then, are involved: the dependence and independence of the composer in relation to historical musical forms. In the first place, the reader may ask: "What are these forms, and why should the composer bother about them in any way?"

The answer to the first part of the question is easy: The sonata-allegro, the variation, the passacaglia, the fugue are the names of some of the best known forms. Each one of these formal molds was only slowly evolved through the combined experience of generations of composers working in many different lands. It would seem foolish for present-day composers to discard all that experience and to begin to work from scratch with each new composition. It is only natural, particularly since the organization of musical material is by its very nature so difficult, that composers tend to lean on these well-tried forms each time that they begin to write. In the back of their minds, before beginning to compose, are all these used and known musical molds which act as a support and, sometimes, a stimulus for their imaginations.

In the same way, a playwright working today, despite the variety of story material at his disposal, generally fits his comedy into the form of a three-act play. That has become the custom—not the five-act play.

Or he may prefer the form of the play in a number of short scenes, which has found favor recently; or the long one-acter without intermission. But whatever he chooses, we presume that he begins from a generalized play form. In the same way, the composer each time begins from a generalized and well-known musical form.

Busoni felt that this was a weakness. He wrote a pamphlet to prove that the future of music demanded the freeing of composers from their overdependence on predetermined forms. Nevertheless, composers continue to depend on them as in the past, and the emergence of a new formal mold is just as rare an occurrence as ever.

But whatever outer mold is chosen, there are certain basic structural principles which must be fulfilled. In other words, no matter what your architectural scheme may be, it must always be psychologically justified by the nature of the material itself. It is that fact which forces the composer out of the formal, given mold.

For example, let us take the case of a composer who is working on a form that generally presupposes a coda, or closing section, at the end of his composition. One day, while working with his material, he happens on a section that he knows was destined to be that coda. It so happens that this particular coda is especially quiet and reminiscent in mood. Just before it, however, a long climax must be built. Now he sets about composing his climax. But by the time he has that long climactic section finished, he may discover that it renders the quiet close superfluous. In such a case, the formal mold will be overthrown, because of the exigencies of the evolving material. Similarly Beethoven, in the first movement of his *Seventh Symphony*, despite what all the textbooks say about "contrasting themes" of the first-movement form, does not have contrasting themes—not in the usual sense, at any rate, owing to the specific character of the thematic material with which he began.

Keep two things in mind, then. Remember the general outlines of the formal mold, and remember that the content of the composer's thought forces him to use that formal mold in a particular and personal way—in a way that belongs only to that particular piece that he is writing. That applies chiefly to art music. Simple folk songs are often of an exactly similar structure within their small frame. But no two symphonies were ever exactly alike.

The prime consideration in all form is the creation of a sense of the *long line* which was mentioned in an earlier chapter. That long line must give us a sense of direction, and we must be made to feel that that direction is the inevitable one. Whatever the means employed, the net result must produce in the listener a satisfying feeling of coherence born out of the psychological necessity of the musical ideas with which the composer began.

STRUCTURAL DISTINCTIONS

There are two ways in which structure in music may be considered: (1) form in relation to a piece as a whole and (2) form in relation to the separate, shorter parts of a piece. The larger formal distinctions would have to do with entire movements of a symphony, a sonata, or a suite. The smaller formal units would together make up one entire movement.

These formal distinctions may be clearer to the layman if an analogy is made with the construction of a novel. A full-length novel might be divided into four books—I, II, III, and IV. That would be analogous to the four movements of a suite or symphony. Book I might be, in turn, divided into five chapters. Similarly, movement I would be made up of five sections. One chapter would contain so many paragraphs. In music, each section would also be subdivided into lesser sections (unfortunately, no special term denotes these smaller units). Paragraphs are composed of sentences.

Musical Structure

In music, the sentence would be analogous to the musical idea. And, of course, the word is analogous to the single musical tone. Needless to say, this comparison is meant to be taken only in a general sense.

In the outlining of a single movement, it has become the custom to represent the larger sections by letters *A, B, C*, etc. Smaller divisions are usually represented by *a, b, c*, etc.

STRUCTURAL PRINCIPLES

One all-important principle is used in music to create the feeling of formal balance. It is so fundamental to the art that it is likely to be used in one way or another as long as music is written. That principle is the very simple one of repetition. The largest part of music bases itself structurally on a broad interpretation of that principle. It seems more justified to use repetition in music than in any of the other arts, probably because of its rather amorphous nature. The only other formal principle that need be mentioned is the opposite of repetition—that is, nonrepetition.

Speaking generally, music that is based on repetition for its spinal structure may be divided into five different categories. The first one is exact repetition; the second, sectional, or symmetrical, repetition; the third, repetition by variation; the fourth, repetition by

fugal treatment; the fifth, repetition through development. Each one of these categories (with the exception
of the first) will receive separate treatment in single
chapters later. Each category will be found to have different type forms which come under the heading of a
specific kind of repetition. Exact repetition (the first
category) is too simple to need any special demonstra-
tion. The other categories are split up according to the
following type forms:

I. Sectional or symmetrical repetition
- a. Two-part (binary) form
- b. Three-part (ternary) form
- c. Rondo
- d. Free sectional arrangement

II. Repetition by variation
- a. Basso ostinato
- b. Passacaglia
- c. Chaconne
- d. Theme and variations

III. Repetition by fugal treatment
- a. Fugue
- b. Concerto grosso
- c. Chorale prelude
- d. Motets and madrigals

IV. Repetition by development
- a. Sonata (first-movement form)

The only other basic formal categories are those
based on nonrepetition, and the so-called "free" forms.

Before launching into discussion of these large type
forms of repetition, it would be wise to examine the principle of repetition applied on a smaller scale. This is eas-

ily done because these repetitional principles apply both to the large sections which comprise an entire movement and also to the small units within each section. Musical form, therefore, resembles a series of wheels within wheels, in which the formation of the smallest wheel is remarkably similar to that of the largest one. A folk song is often constructed on lines similar to one of these smaller units and whenever possible will be used to illustrate the simplest repetition principles.

The most elementary of all is that of exact repetition, which may be represented by *a-a-a-a*, etc. Such simple repetitions are to be found in many songs, where the same music is repeated for consecutive stanzas. The first form of variation occurs when, in similar songs, minor alterations are made in the repetition to allow for a closer setting of the text. This kind of repetition may be represented as *a-a'-a"-a'"*, etc.

The next form of repetition is fundamental not only to many folk songs but also to art music in its smallest and largest sections. It is repetition after a digression. This repetition may be exact, in which case it is represented by *a-b-a*; or it may be varied and therefore represented by *a-b-a'*. Very often in music the first *a* is immediately repeated. There would appear to be some fundamental need to impress a first phrase or section on the listener's mind before the digression comes. Most theorists agree, however, that the essential *a-b-a* form is unchanged by the repetition of the first *a*. (In music, it is possible to indicate the repetition by the sign :‖, making the formula ‖: *a* :‖-*b-a*.) Here is this species of repetition in two folk songs, *Au clair de la lune* and *Ach! du lieber Augustin:*

Au clair de la lune

Ach! du lieber Augustin

Musical Structure

The very same formula may be found in art music. The first of Schumann's piano pieces in *Scenes from Childhood* is a good example of a short piece made up of *a-b-a*, with the first *a* repeated. Here is the melodic line without the accompaniment:

The same formula, with slight changes, may be found as part of a longer piece in the first page of the Scherzo from Beethoven's *Piano Sonata*, Op. 27, No. 2. Here, even the first *a* when immediately repeated, is slightly changed by a certain dislocation in the rhythm; and the final repetition is different by a stronger cadential feeling at the end. (A "cadence" in music means a closing phrase.) Here is the melodic outline:

Allegretto

It would be easy to multiply examples of the *a-b-a* formula, with tiny variations, but my purpose is not to be all-inclusive. The point to remember about these smaller units is that every time a theme is exposed, there is strong likelihood that it will be repeated immediately; that once repeated, a digression is in order; and that after the digression, a return to the first theme, either exact or varied, is to be expected. How this same *a-b-a* formula applies to a piece as a whole, including the sonata form, will be demonstrated in later chapters.

The only other basic formal principle, that of nonrepetition, may be represented by the formula *a-b-c-d*, etc. It may be illustrated in a small way by the following English folk song *The Seeds of Love*, all four phrases of which are different:

This same principle may be found in many of the preludes composed by Bach and other of his contemporaries. A short example is the B flat major Prelude from Book I of the *Well Tempered Clavichord*. Unity is achieved by adopting a specific pattern, writing freely within that pattern, but avoiding any repetition of notes or phrases. We shall be returning to it in the chapter on Free Forms.

To obtain a similar unity in a piece lasting twenty minutes without using any form of thematic repetition is no easy achievement. That probably accounts for the fact that the principle of nonrepetition is applied for the most part to short compositions. The listener will find it used much less frequently than any of the repetition forms, which now must be considered in detail.

10

Fundamental Forms

I · SECTIONAL FORM

Two Part; Three Part; Rondo;
Free Sectional Arrangement

THE easiest form for the listener to grasp is that built sectionally. The more or less clearly defined separation of related parts is readily assimilated. From a certain perspective, practically all music might be considered to be sectionally constructed—even the long tone poems of a Richard Strauss. But in this chapter we shall confine ourselves to those type forms which are obviously made up of a combination in some arrangement of separate sections.

TWO-PART FORM

The simplest of these is two-part, or binary, form, represented by *A-B*. Two-part form is very little used nowadays, but it played a preponderant role in the music written from 1650 to 1750. The division into *A* and *B* may be clearly seen on the printed page, for the end of the *A* section is almost always indicated by a double bar with a repetition sign. Sometimes a repetition sign follows the end of the *B* section also, in which case the formula would more truly be *A-A-B-B*. But, as I have already pointed out, in analyzing forms we do not take into account these exact repetitions, because they do not really affect the general outlines of the music as a whole. Moreover, interpreters use their own discretion in the matter of actually playing the repetitions indicated.

In all other forms, a *B* section would indicate an independent section, different in musical material from the *A* section. In two-part form, however, there is a general correspondence between the first and second parts. The *A* and *B* seem to balance one another; *B* often is little more than a rearranged version of *A*. Exactly how the "rearrangement" is carried out differs

Sectional Form

with each piece and largely accounts for the great variety within the two-part structure. The B section is often made up partly of a repetition of A, and partly of a kind of development of certain phrases to be found in A. It might be said, therefore, that the principle of development which became so important in later times had its origin here. The two parts of the form will be clearly heard by the layman if he listens for the strong cadential feeling at the end of each part.

The two-part form was utilized in thousands of short pieces for clavecin, written during the seventeenth and eighteenth centuries. The seventeenth-century type of suite was comprised of four or five or more of such pieces, which were in some species of dance form. The dances most usually included in the suite are the allemande, the courante, the saraband, and the gigue. Not so often used are the gavotte, bourrée, passepied, and louré. (This early type of suite is not to be confused with the modern suite which is nothing more than a collection of pieces lighter in character than the movements of a sonata or symphony.)

As examples of two-part form, the reader is urged to hear pieces by François Couperin or Domenico Scarlatti. (Recordings by Wanda Landowska of both composers are recommended.) Couperin, who lived from 1668 to 1733, published four books of clavecin pieces, containing some of the finest music ever written by a Frenchman. They often are titled fancifully, for example, *The Mysterious Barricades* or *Twins* or *The Little Fly*. This last piece (*Le Moucheron*) is a particularly fine example of two-part form. So is *La Commère*, which is, besides, a brilliant example of eighteenth-century wit and *esprit*. Something of the sensuosity of present-day French music will be found in *Les langeurs tendres*. Couperin created a world of subtle feeling within the limits of this miniature form.

Domenico Scarlatti (1685–1757) is the Italian counterpart of Couperin. He composed hundreds of pieces in two-part form, all under the generic name of sonata, though they have nothing in common with the later sonata either in form or in feeling. Scarlatti's personality is strongly evident in everything he wrote. He had a penchant for brilliant, showy clavecin writing, with large skips and crossing of hands in true instrumental style. Nor was he afraid of using harmonies that must have struck his contemporaries as daring. (Many of these harmonies were "toned down" by academic editors of the nineteenth century.) It is difficult to choose examples from so great a profusion of riches. In the Longo edition, *Sonatas* No. 413 (D minor), No. 104 (C major), and No. 338 (G minor) are among his finest works.

Sectional Form

The second type of sectional form is three-part form, represented by the formula *A-B-A*. We have already seen how the small unit of a piece may be built according to *a-b-a*. Now it is necessary to demonstrate it in relation to a piece as a whole.

THREE-PART FORM

In the case of three-part form, we are dealing with a type of construction that is in continual use by composers today. Among the clearest early examples are the minuets of Haydn or Mozart. Here the *B* section—sometimes labeled "trio"—is in distinct contrast to the *A* section. It is sometimes almost like an independent little piece, bounded on both sides by the first part: minuet-trio-minuet. When the return to the first section was exact repetition, composers did not trouble to write it out again but merely indicated "da capo" (from the beginning). But when the return is varied, the third section must be written out.

The minuet, and with it the three-part form, gradually changed its character, even among so-called classical composers. Haydn himself began the transformation of the minuet from a simple dance form to what finally became the Beethoven scherzo. In fact, there are few better examples of the gradual expansion of a formal pattern than this metamorphosis of minuet to

[131]

scherzo. The outline *A-B-A* remained the same, but the character became transformed completely. In Beethoven's hands, the graceful and dignified minuet turned into the brusque and whimsical scherzo-allegro which contrasts so well with the slow preceding movement.

One important alteration was made in the form by Beethoven himself and adopted by composers who followed him. It was usual to have, in the earlier minuets and scherzos, a complete sense of close at the end of both first and second parts. Later examples of the form, however, connect the *A* section by a bridge passage to the *B* section; and likewise, on the return, *B* to *A*, thereby creating a greater impression of continuity. This tendency will be found in most forms in music; the demarcation points of separate sections tend to melt away before the need for a greater impression of continuous flow. Definitely marked divisions are easier to follow from the listener's vantage point, but the higher development of form brings with it the need for the manipulation of an uninterrupted and longer line.

Here is a typical illustration of the Haydn Minuet from the *String Quartet*, Op. 17, No. 5. The divisions are clearly marked:

[132]

Sectional Form

Attacca il Menuetto

For a modern example of minuet form, I can recommend the Ravel Minuet from *Le tombeau de Couperin*,
a set of six piano pieces, which were later orchestrated
by the composer. The typical *A-B-A* form is present,
with these differences: The return to the *A* section is
made up of an ingenious combination of both *A* and *B*
at the same time; and a fairly elaborate coda is added
at the end. But nothing essential to the form of the
minuet has been changed.

Now let us see what Beethoven did with the minuet

[134]

form. Let us take as illustration the same Scherzo from the *Piano Sonata*, Op. 27, No. 2, the first page of which was analyzed in the preceding chapter. In analyzing the Scherzo as a whole, that first page, which itself was found to be ‖:*a*:‖ -*b*-*a*, counts as *A* of the larger *A-B-A* formula. The *B* section—the Trio—is more sustained in quality, for the sake of contrast. This is almost always true of any middle part of a scherzo and makes the divisions easily distinguishable. The return to the *A* is an exact repetition.

Played slowly, this particular Scherzo might conceivably be a minuet, but that is not true of the Scherzo of the *Sonata*, Op. 27, No. 1. The Beethoven-like, stormy character completely removes it from the stately minuet that originated the form. To have written a *B* section of the usual sustained and contrasted type would have dissipated the mood of the *A* section. It is interesting to see how Beethoven manages both to write a contrasting section and yet to keep up the hectic, seething character of the first part. The return to the *A* is varied by a slight syncopation in the rhythm, which serves to emphasize the stormy mood.

Three-part form, with slight adaptations, is the generic type form for innumerable pieces, variously named. Some of the most familiar are: nocturne, berceuse, reverie, ballade, elegy, waltz, étude, capriccio,

impromptu, intermezzo, mazurka, polonaise, etc. These
are not, of course, necessarily three-part in form, but
they certainly are likely to be. Always watch for the
contrasted middle part and some kind of return to the
beginning. Those are the unmistakable earmarks of the
three-part form.

Limitation of space forbids the pointing out of more
than one illustration: the Chopin *Prelude* No. 15, in D
flat. This is an excellent example of "adaptation" of
the *A-B-A* form. After a first part of quiet and sustained mood comes the *B* part, which is more dramatic
and "threatening," by way of contrast. It demonstrates
a tendency, which later became more and more fre-
quent, to find a way of connecting the *B* to the *A* by
utilizing some element common to both, such as a
rhythmic or melodic figure (in this case, a repeated
note). Treated thus, the *B* section seems to grow out
of the first part instead of being merely an independent and contrasted section, which might conceivably
belong to some other piece equally well. The return
to the *A* in this *Prelude* is very much shortened. It is as
if Chopin said to the listener: "You remember the mood
of this first part. Taking you back for a few measures
will suffice to give you a feeling of the whole without
bothering to play it all the way through." That is good
psychological reasoning in this particular piece and

adds to both the originality and the conciseness of the formal treatment.

THE RONDO

The third important type form which bases itself on the sectional principle is that of the rondo. It is easily reduced to the formula *A-B-A-C-A-D-A*, etc. The typical feature of any rondo, therefore, is the return to the principal theme after every digression. The main theme is the important thing; the number or length of the digressions is immaterial. The digressions provide contrast and balance; that is their principal function. There are different types of rondo form, both slow and fast. But the most usual type is that found as final movement of a sonata—light, cheerful, and songlike.

The rondo is a very old musical form, but it has far from outlived its usefulness. Examples may be found in the music of Couperin as well as in the latest work of the American Walter Piston. In early examples— even up to and including the time of Haydn and Mozart—the divisions between sections were clearly marked. But here, again, later developments in the use of the form tend to break down demarkation points, so that one may truthfully say that the essential quality of the rondo is the creation of an uninterrupted sense of flow. That smoothly flowing style is fundamental to the rondo character, whether the music is old or new.

A fine illustration of the early rondo is the outline of the last movement of the Haydn *Piano Sonata*, No. 9, in D major (see pages 139–141). Notice a very important feature, the fact that each time the *A* returns, it is varied, which makes for new interest despite the numerous repetitions. Later rondos invariably show different versions of *A* each time that it returns.

Numerous examples of modern rondos will be found in the works of Roussel, Milhaud, Hindemith, Stravinsky, Schoenberg, etc. The famous example from Strauss, *Till Eulenspiegel's Merry Pranks*, is too complex to be grasped without special analysis.

FREE SECTIONAL FORM

The fourth, and final, type of sectional build-up cannot be reduced to any one formula, because it allows for any free arrangement of sections which together make a coherent whole. Any arrangement that makes musical sense is possible, for instance *A-B-B* or *A-B-C-A* or *A-B-A-C-A-B-A*. The first is the formula of the Chopin *Prelude in C minor*, No. 20; the last is that of the piece called *Frightening* from Schumann's *Scenes from Childhood*. It is particularly easy to follow in the

Sectional Form

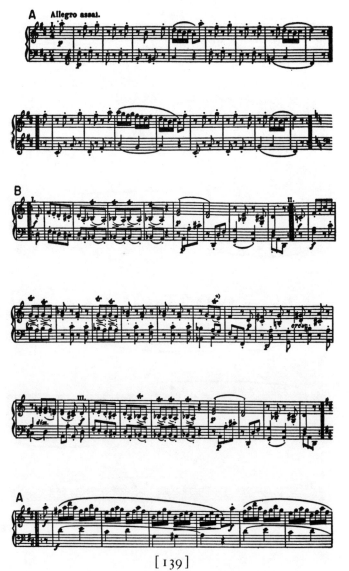

TO A VARIED

Sectional Form

Schumann piece, because each section is so short and so different in character.

A good example of an unconventional arrangement of various sections, as used by a modern composer, is Béla Bartók's *Suite*, Op. 14, in the first and second movements.

Fundamental Forms

II · VARIATION FORM

Basso Ostinato; Passacaglia; Chaconne;
Theme and Variations

THE variation forms well exemplify what the listener is expected to hear and what he is not expected to hear, as regards form in music. That is to say, it would be foolish to imagine that any listener, when hearing a variation form for the first time, hears it with any degree of exactitude as regards each separate variation. Nevertheless, it is of considerable value to him to know the general outlines, even though he is unable to follow the working out of each individual variation in detail. With a little preparation, it is comparatively easy to hear the general outlines of any variation form, whether the work is that of a classic or that of a modern composer.

Before going further, the reader should be warned that the variation in music has two different aspects and that they must not be confused. The first aspect is that of the variation used as a device in music, in a purely incidental way. That is, any of the elements in music may be varied—any harmony, any melody, any rhythm. Likewise, the variation as a device may be applied momentarily to any form—sectional, sonata, fugal, etc. It is a device so fundamental, in fact, that composers fall back on it continuously and apply it almost without thinking. But the second aspect must not be lost sight of—the variation as used in the different variation forms proper, where it is the sole and exclusive formal principle. It is this second aspect that I propose to treat here.

The principle of variation in music is a very old one. It belongs to the art so naturally that it would be hard to imagine a time when it was not being used. Even in Palestrina's day, and before, when vocal music was paramount, the principle of varying a melody was well established in musical practice. A Mass by a sixteenth-century master was often based entirely on a single melody which was used in a varied form in each of the separate parts of the Mass. Though the variation principle was first applied melodically, the English virginal composers soon adapted it to instrumental style by varying the harmonic framework in much the same way that it is done nowadays. In fact, these early English masters used this new device to such an extent that it became rather tiresome; it became not so much a formal principle as a mere formula. Anybody could take a theme and write ten variations on it full of runs and trills and a profusion of figurations, which were not in themselves overly interesting. Naturally, that isn't true of the best examples of the period, such as Byrd's variations on *The Carman's Whistle*.

Since that time there has hardly been a period during which composers have not written in the variation form. As a basic mold it was repeatedly used by the classical Haydn and Mozart, the early romantics Beethoven and Schubert, and the later romanticists Schumann and Brahms. It flourishes today, as ever, as witness the famous *Don Quixote* of Strauss, the *Enigma Variations* of Elgar, the *Istar Variations* of D'Indy, or to come to more recent times, the *Octet* of Stravinsky, the *Schwanendreher* of Hindemith, the string quartet (*Three Variations on a Theme*) of Roy Harris. This should be

Variation Form

proof, if proof were needed, that the variation forms are fundamental in musical history; and it is unlikely that composers will ever completely abandon them.

BASSO OSTINATO

Of the four types of variation forms, the basso ostinato, or ground bass, is the easiest to recognize. It might more properly be termed a musical device than a musical form. Literally translated, it means an "obstinate bass," which is more or less an exact description of what it is. A short phrase—either an accompanimental figure or an actual melody—is repeated over and over again in the bass part, while the upper parts proceed normally. It provides an easy method for writing "modern music" of the 1920 vintage, the left hand continuing always in the same way, and the right hand left to its own devices. Perhaps because of that, for a time the basso ostinato exerted too strong a charm on the newer composers.

Now let us examine illustrations of the basso ostinato as it was practiced at different periods. The simplest versions are those in which the ground bass is little more than an accompanimental figure. The *Pastorale* for piano of Sibelius presents such a figure:*

*From *From the Land of a Thousand Lakes*, by Jean Sibelius. Used by permission of The Boston Music Company.

Another, and more recent, example is the *Cortège* from Arthur Honegger's well-known oratorio *King David*.* Here, too, the ostinato bass is a mere figure,

which lends itself well to the piquant tonal changes of
the upper part:

Note that once the ground bass is firmly established
in your consciousness, it may, to a certain extent, be
taken for granted, thereby permitting a greater concentration on the remaining material.

What to Listen for in Music

Many beautiful illustrations may be culled from music of the seventeenth century. Here is one from Monteverdi's last works, written in 1642, *The Coronation of Poppea*. In this case, the ground bass is no

longer a mere figure; it is a real melody in its own right.

Henry Purcell, one of the greatest composers England has ever produced, lived toward the end of the seventeenth century and was especially fond of the basso ostinato. His works show numerous illustrations of the most varied use of this device. Here is an example taken from his famous opera *Dido and Aeneas*, a solo song called "Dido's Lament." The ground bass is

surprisingly chromatic and therefore easy to remember, and the chords above it have a romantic glow about them far in advance of Purcell's period.

One of the best of modern examples is the second number called the "Soldier's Violin" from Stravinsky's pantomime *The Story of a Soldier*. With the aid of four notes pizzicato in the double bass, the composer pens a half-pitiful, half-sarcastic picture which provides one of the earliest and best illustrations of humor in modern music. [Felix Petyrek makes effective use of the basso ostinato for humorous purposes in his *Eleven Small Children's Pieces* (no recording available).]

THE PASSACAGLIA

The passacaglia is the second type of variation form. Here, again, as in the basso ostinato, an entire composition is founded upon a repeated bass part. But this time, the ground bass is invariably a melodic phrase, never a mere figure. It is also open to more varied treatment, as we shall soon see, than the literal repetitions of the basso ostinato.

The origin of the passacaglia is not too well known. It is said to have been a slow dance, in three-quarter time, of Spanish origin. At any rate, the present-day passacaglia, and those of the past, are always slow and dignified in character, retaining the original three-

Variation Form

quarter time signature, although not invariably so. But all connection with the dance has been lost.

A passacaglia invariably begins with a statement of the theme unaccompanied, in the bass. Since it is this theme that is to form the foundation for all further variation, it is of paramount importance that the theme itself be well established in the mind of the listener. Therefore, as a rule, for the first few variations the theme is literally repeated in the bass, while the upper part begins a gentle forward movement.

Speaking generally, the composer has two objectives in treating the passacaglia form. First, with the addition of each new variation the theme must be seen in a new light. In other words, interest in the oft repeated ground bass must be aroused and sustained and added to by the composer's creative imagination. Secondly, aside from the beauty of any one variation, taken alone, they must all together gather cumulative momentum, so that the form as a whole may be psychologically satisfying. This second objective has been particularly true since Bach's time.

The literal repetitions of the theme in the bass need not be retained after the first few variations. The simplest device is to move the theme itself to an upper or middle part, inverting its natural position. Other devices momentarily conceal the theme, though it is

surely present either as the bottom note of some figuration or as the bottom note of what may appear to
be a mere chordal accompaniment. The theme played
twice as slowly or twice as fast or contrapuntally combined with new thematic material is in each case a le-
gitimate device for variation possibilities.

In binding the different variations into a coherent
whole, it is customary to group several variations of a
similar pattern together. This affords smoother tran-
sitions from one type of variation to the next. Cumulative effect has often been achieved, from Bach's time
onward, by the simple process of increasing the number of notes in a measure, thereby creating a sense of
climax through faster and faster motion. As a matter
of fact, one of the main differences between Bach's use
of the form and that of his predecessors was this adop-
tion of a faster and faster motion to build climaxes, a
device that has since been used over and over again
and not only in the passacaglia form.

One of the finest examples in all musical literature,
and one which is invariably quoted when the form is
under discussion, is Bach's great organ *Passacaglia* in C
minor. It is based on the following characteristic theme:

Variation Form

The lay listener is urged to study the notes or the recording or both many times, as few compositions will better repay careful listening. First, it is necessary to have the theme well in mind. Then to remember that a new variation begins each time the theme has been played through once. This may cause confusion at first, when, as in the first two variations, the pattern is almost identical, except for a heightening of the expressive harmonies in the second. Note how the movement begins to get faster in the fourth variation, changing from eighth notes to sixteenths. For the first four variations the theme remains exactly the same; in the fifth variation the theme, in a disguised version, may be found as the bottom note of each upward arpeggio. In the eighth variation, a new contrapuntal line is added above chords, the bottom note of which is thematic. In the next variation, the theme is transposed to the soprano part, with the contrapuntal line below it. Note particularly the gathering momentum at the end, just before the fugue begins. (Fugues are often written as the conclusion of a passacaglia, but they do not affect the form itself in any way.)

The passacaglia was somewhat neglected during the nineteenth century. Composers during that period seemed to prefer writing the theme and variations when treating variation forms. But modern composers have written passacaglias. A good example is that of the middle movement of the Ravel *Trio* for violin, cello, and piano. Both Alban Berg in his opera *Wozzeck* and Anton Webern (*Passacaglia* for orchestra, Op. 1) show modern treatments of the form.

THE CHACONNE

The chaconne is the third type of variation form. It is very closely related to the passacaglia. In fact, the differences are so slight, that at times there has been considerable argument among theorists as to whether to label a piece a passacaglia or a chaconne, if the composer himself neglected to do so. The classic example of that is the last movement of Brahms' *Fourth Symphony*. Some commentators refer to it as a passacaglia, and others as a chaconne. Since Brahms called it only the fourth movement, the argument will probably continue for a long time to come.

In any case, the chaconne, like the passacaglia, was in all likelihood originally a slow dance form in three-quarter time. It still retains its stately, sober character. But unlike the passacaglia, it does not begin with an unaccompanied bass theme. Instead, the bass theme is heard from the start with accompanying harmonies. This means that the bass theme is not given the ex-

Variation Form

clusively important role to play that it occupies in the passacaglia; for the accompanying harmonies are also sometimes varied in the chaconne. So that the chaconne is a kind of stepping stone between the passacaglia and the theme and variations, as will appear presently.

Here is a chaconne theme from the great forerunner of Bach's, Dietrich Buxtehude:

In this case, as you see, the theme in the bass already has its accompanying harmonies, so that this first statement sounds as if it were the first variation of a passacaglia. That is where the confusion begins.

The great modern example of the chaconne form is the movement of the Brahms symphony mentioned above, for it is in that category that I myself should list it. Unfortunately, space limitations prevent any detailed analysis. Suffice it to say that the theme which later constitutes the ground bass is first heard as the top part of the opening chords, which are themselves retained along with the theme in many instances. In other words, the chaconne, unlike the passacaglia, has something of a harmonic bias along with its ground bass.

THEME AND VARIATIONS

The theme and variations is the last, and most important, of the variation forms. Its fame has spread beyond the realm of absolute music, something in the manner of the fugue form, and has been used to title poems and novels.

The theme that is adopted for variation is either original with the composer or borrowed from some other source. As a rule, the theme itself is simple and direct in character. It is best to have it so in order that the listener may hear it in its simplest version before the

[156]

Variation Form

varying process begins. The reader must keep in mind the fact that the theme and variations, like many other forms, became increasingly complex as time went on. In the earlier examples, the theme was usually in a clearly defined small two- or three-part form, the outlines of which were retained in each variation that followed. The separate variations themselves, on the other hand, were loosely strung together, seeming to possess as formal principle only a general sense of balance and contrast.

Modern practice reverses this. The outlines of the theme with which the composer begins are often lost sight of in each separate variation, but a definite attempt is made to build all of them together into some semblance of structural unity. What was stated in this connection in relation to passacaglia form—the joining of the separate parts in view of their cumulative effect—is even more true of the theme and variations.

There are different types of variation which may be applied to practically any theme. Five general types may easily be distinguished: (1) harmonic, (2) melodic, (3) rhythmic, (4) contrapuntal, (5) a combination of all four previous types. No textbook formula could possibly foresee every kind of variation scheme that an inventive composer might hit upon. It is even difficult to illustrate the five main divisions I have chosen from any one piece. For purposes of illustration it seemed better to write out the beginnings of typical variation schemes for some well-known tune, such as *Ach! du lieber Augustin* (see Appendix I).

As has already been said, this by no means exhausts the almost limitless possibilities for the variation of any single theme. It is customary with most composers to stay rather close to the original theme at the beginning of a composition, taking more and more liberties as the piece progresses. Very often, at the very end, the theme is stated once again in its original form. It is as if the composer were saying: "You see how far away it was possible to go; well, here we are back again where we started."

Musical literature is so generously supplied with themes and variations that the mentioning of any particular example would seem almost superfluous. Nevertheless, I strongly advise the reader to hear the first movement of Mozart's A major *Piano Sonata*, which is in the form of a theme and six variations. Note that the formal outline of the theme is retained in each of the six variations. Variation I is a good example of the florid-melodic type of variation; variation 4, of the skeltonizing of the harmony. One small device, dear to the classic masters, is exemplified by the third variation, where the harmony is changed from major to minor. From the listener's standpoint, it is important to be conscious of the beginning of each new variation, so that the piece is split up in your mind in the same way that it was divided in the composer's mind at the moment of composition.

Excellent nineteenth century examples, but of a much greater complexity than the Mozart, are Schumann's much quoted *Etudes Symphoniques* and the less well-known but admirable *Theme and Variations* of Gabriel Fauré.

An interesting modern example, containing a slight variation of the variation form itself, is the middle movement of Stravinsky's *Octet*. Here, instead of the usual scheme: $A\text{-}A'\text{-}A''\text{-}A'''\text{-}A''''$, etc., we get this plan: $A\text{-}A'\text{-}A''\text{-}A'\text{-}A'''\text{-}A''''\text{-}A'\text{-}A$. The curious feature here is that the composer, after a few variations, does not return each time to the theme itself (as in the rondo form) but to the first variation of the theme.

The author's own *Piano Variations* (1930), based on a comparatively short theme, reverses the usual procedure by putting the simplest version of the theme second, calling what is, properly speaking, a first variation a "theme." The idea was to present the listener with a more striking version of the theme first, which seemed more in keeping with the generally dramatic character of the composition as a whole.

[159]

12

Fundamental Forms

III · FUGAL FORM

*Fugue; Concerto Grosso; Chorale
Prelude; Motets and Madrigals*

CHAPTER 1 began from the premise that it was essential, in learning to listen more intelligently, to hear a great deal of music over and over again; and that no amount of reading could possibly replace that listening. What was written there is especially true in regard to fugal forms. If you really wish to hear what goes on in these forms, you must be willing to go after them again and again. More than any other formal

[160]

Fugal Form

mold, fugal forms demand repeated hearings if they are to be fully heard by the layman.

Whatever comes under the heading of fugal form partakes in some way of the nature of a fugue. You already know, I feel sure, that in texture all fugues are polyphonic or contrapuntal (the terms are identical in meaning). Therefore, it follows that all fugal forms are polyphonic or contrapuntal in texture.

At this point, the reader might do well to review what was said in Chapter 8 about listening polyphonically. It was stated there that hearing music polyphonically implies a listener who can hear separate strands of melody simultaneously. The parts need not be of equal importance, but they must be heard independently. This is no great feat; any person of average intelligence can, with a little practice, hear more than one melody at a time. At any rate, it is the *sine qua non* of intelligent listening to fugal forms.

The four principal fugal forms are: first, the fugue proper; second, the concerto grosso; third, the chorale-prelude; fourth, motets and madrigals. It goes without saying that contrapuntal writing is not confined to these forms alone. Just as the principle of variation was seen to be applicable to any form, so in the same way a contrapuntal texture may occur without preparation in almost any form. Be ready, in other words, to listen polyphonically at any moment.

A certain number of well-known contrapuntal devices are used whenever the texture is polyphonic. They are not invariably present, but they may put in an appearance, and so the listener must be on the lookout for them. The simplest of these devices are: imitation, canon, inversion, augmentation, diminution. More recondite are cancrizans (crab motion) and the inverted cancrizans. Some of these devices, enmeshed within the web of contrapuntal texture, are quite difficult to follow. I point them out now more for the sake of completeness than because you will learn from one single illustration to recognize them each time that they occur (see Appendix II).

Imitation is the simplest device of all. Anyone who has ever sung a round in school will know the meaning of imitation. Playing a kind of "follow-the-leader" musical game, one voice imitates what another voice does. When used incidentally during the course of a piece, this device is referred to as "imitation." This perfectly natural idea may be found in very early music as well as in contemporary music. The simplest imitation sets up an illusion of many-voiced music, although only one melody is actually sounded. The imitation need not start on the same note with which the original voice begins. In such a case, we speak of

Fugal Form

imitation "at the fourth" above or "at the second" below, indicating the pitch at which the entrance of the imitating voice was made. Paradoxically, you have to listen contrapuntally, although only one melody is in question.

Canon is merely a more elaborate species of imitation, in which the imitation is carried out logically from the beginning of a piece to the end. In other words, canon may be spoken of as a form, whereas imitation is always a device. Eighteenth-century music supplies numerous examples; the most quoted illustration of the past century is that of the last movement of César Franck's *Violin Sonata*. Recently, Hindemith has written canons in the form of sonatas for two flutes.

Inversion is not so easily recognized. It consists of turning a melody upside down, as it were. The melody inverted always moves in the opposite direction from the melody in its original version. That is, when the original leaps an octave upward, the inversion leaps an octave downward, and so forth. Of course, not all melodies make sense when inverted. It is up to the composer to decide whether or not the inversion of a melody is justified on musical grounds.

Augmentation is easily explained. When you augment a theme, you double the time value of the notes,

[163]

thereby making the theme twice as slow as it originally was. (A quarter note becomes a half, a half note a whole, etc.) Diminution is the opposite of augmentation. It consists of halving the note values, so that the theme moves twice as fast as originally. (A whole note becomes a half, a half note a quarter, etc.)

Cancrizans, or crab motion, as the name implies, means the melody read backward. In other words, *A-B-C-D* becomes, in cancrizans, *D-C-B-A*. Here, again, the mere mechanical application of the device does not always produce musical results. Cancrizans is much more rarely found than the other contrapuntal devices, although the modern Viennese school, led by Arnold Schoenberg, has made liberal use of it. Still more involved is inverted cancrizans, in which the theme is first read backward and then inverted.

The ability to listen contrapuntally, plus a comprehension of these various devices, is all that is necessary in order to prepare oneself to hear fugues intelligently. Most fugues are written in three or four voices. Five-voiced fugues are rarer, and two-voiced rarer still. Once a certain number of voices are adopted, they are held to throughout. They are not, however, continuously present in the fugue, for a well-written fugue implies breathing spaces in each melodic line.

Fugal Form

So that in a four-voiced fugue, the listener seldom hears more than three voices at a time.

But no matter how many voices may be going on at the same time, there is always one voice that predominates. Just as a juggler, handling three objects, draws our attention to the object that goes highest, so, in the same way, the composer draws our attention to one of the equally independent voices. It is the theme, or subject, of the fugue that takes precedence whenever present. Therefore, the reader can appreciate how important it is to bear in mind the subject of the fugue. Composers aid by invariably stating the subject at the beginning of the fugue without accompaniment. Fugue subjects are generally rather short—two or three measures long—and of a well-defined character. (Examine, if you can, the famous forty-eight fugue themes used by Bach in his *Well Tempered Clavichord*.)

Before demonstrating as much as can be blue-printed of the fugue as a whole, it should be made clear that the general outlines of the form are not nearly so definite as that of other formal molds. Every fugue differs as to presentation of voices, as to length, and as to inner detail. Its separate parts are not nearly so distinguishable as, let us say, separate parts in sectional forms. In a nontechnical book of this sort, it is not possible to make the measure-by-measure explanation that each fugue demands for complete analysis.

All fugues, however, begin with what is called an "exposition." Let us see what the exposition of a fugue consists of before going on to examine the remainder of the form. Every fugue, as I have said, begins with an announcement of the unadorned fugue subject. If we take as model a four-voiced fugue, then the subject will appear for the first time in one of four voices: soprano, alto, tenor, or bass. (For convenience sake, let's call them V-1, V-2, V-3, and V-4.) Any one of the four voices may have the first statement of the fugue subject. Whatever the order may be, the subject is heard in each one of the four voices, one after another, like this:

```
V-1   S...........
V-2                S..........
V-3                          S..........
V-4                                    S..........
```

Or the order of entrance may be thus:

```
V-1                                    S..........
V-2                          S..........
V-3   S.........
V-4                                    S..........
```

(V-2 and V-4 are more exactly known as "answers" to the subject. I have retained "subject" in all four voices for the sake of simplicity.)

It goes without saying that when the second voice

enters with the subject, the first voice does not stop. On the contrary, it continues to add a countermelody, or countersubject as it is generally called (CS), to the principal subject. Thus, the ground plan really reads:

```
V-1    S.......CS........
V-2            S.......CS.......
V-3                    S......CS.......
V-4                            S......CS.......
```

When once the subject and countersubject are exposed in any one voice, it is free to continue without restrictions as a so-called "free voice." With that filled in, our ground plan of the exposition is completed:

```
V-1    S......CS......xxFV......xx..................
V-2            S......xxCS......xxFV...............
V-3                    S......xxCS.......FV......
V-4                            S.......CS......
```

In some fugues, it is not feasible to go directly from one entrance of a voice to the next without a measure or two of transition, because of tonal relationships too technical to be gone into here. That is what the crosses indicate. The exposition is considered to be at an end when each of the voices of a fugue has sung the theme once. (Certain fugues have a reexposition section in which the exposition is repeated but with the voices entering in different order.)

The exposition is the only part of the fugue form

that is definitely set. From there on, the form can be summarized only loosely. The general plan might be reduced to a formula something like this: exposition—(reexposition)—episode 1—subject—episode 2—subject—episode 3—subject—(etc.)—stretto (see page 169 for explanation of this term)—cadence. Speaking generally, a series of episodes alternate with statements of the fugue subject, seen each time in new aspects. No rules govern the number of episodes or returns of the theme. An episode is often related to some fragment of the fugue subject or countersubject. It seldom is made up entirely of independent materials. Its principal function is to divert attention from the theme of the fugue, so as better to prepare the stage for its reentrance. Its general character is usually that of a bridge section—more relaxed in quality, less dialectic than the fugue subject developments.

Despite the appearance of the preceding formula, there is no actual repetition in a fugue except for the kernel of the fugue subject itself, and the countersubject which often accompanies its every appearance. Half the point of fugue form would be missed if it were not clearly understood that with each entrance of the fugue subject a different light is thrown upon the theme itself. It may be augmented or inverted, combined with itself or with other new themes, shortened or length-

Fugal Form

ened, sung quietly or boldly. Each new appearance tests the ingenuity of the composer. During the main body of the fugue—that is, after the exposition and before the stretto—a severe modulatory scheme is generally adopted, which is too technical for full discussion here.

A stretto in a fugue is optional, but when present it is usually found just before the final cadence. Stretto is the name given a species of imitation in which the separate parts enter so immediately one after another that an impression of toppling voices is obtained. Not all fugue subjects lend themselves equally well to this kind of treatment, which explains why strettos are not found in every fugue. Whatever the nature of the fugue, the end is never casual. It brings with it, as a rule, one final, clear statement of the fugue subject and an insistence on the establishment without question of the tonic key.

The fugue asks for concentrated listening and is therefore not very long, a few pages at most. The character of the fugue is limited only by the imagination of its creator. It may be somber or witty, but it never tries to be both in one fugue. As far as its general character goes, a fugue says one thing, and it derives its keynote from the nature of the fugue subject itself. The emotional scope, in other words, is limited to the kind of theme with which one begins.

The disciplinary aspect of the fugue has challenged the ingenuity of composers for centuries and continues to do so. But the consensus of opinion is that the fugue, in essence, is an eighteenth-century form. That may be partly accounted for by the fact that the composers of the following century tended to neglect a form that was undoubtedly associated in their minds with the formalism of a past era, plus the emphasis placed upon freedom of expression during the romantic period. There were other reasons also, but these will suffice.

Recent composers, however, have shown a renewal of interest in the fugue. Whether or not their accomplishments in this field will justify their redoing a form that the past has done so consummately well, the future alone can tell. In any case, there is nothing essentially different about a modern fugue. As far as the form goes, or the general emotional character, it is still the fugue of a disciplined age. The listener's problem is exactly similar in both cases.

CONCERTO GROSSO

The second principal fugal form is that of the concerto grosso. It, too, is an essentially prenineteenthcentury form, as are all these fugal forms. It should not be confused in your mind with the later concerto, which is written for a virtuoso soloist accompanied by orchestra. The origin of the concerto grosso is attributable to the fact that composers in the second half of the seventeenth century became intrigued by the effect to be obtained from contrasting a small body of instruments with a large body of instruments. The smaller group, called the concertino, might be formed of any combination of instruments pleasing to the composer. Whatever the smaller group of instruments may be, the form is built around the dialectical interchange between the concertino and the larger body of instruments, or tutti, as it is often called.

The concerto grosso, then, is a kind of instrumental fugal form. It is generally made up of three or more movements. The classical examples of the form are those of Handel and Bach. The latter's essays in the form, known as the *Brandenburg Concerti*, of which there are six, make use of a different concertino in each one. Very often, in listening to the contrapuntal texture of one of these works, one has an impression of wonderful health and vitality. The inner movement of the separate parts gives off an athletic quality, as if all were in excellent working order.

During the nineteenth century, the form was abandoned in favor of the concerto for soloist and orchestra, which may rightfully be considered an offshoot of the earlier concerto grosso. Like other eighteenth-century forms, the concerto grosso has enjoyed renewed interest on the part of recent composers. A well-known modern example is the *Concerto Grosso* by Ernest Bloch.

CHORALE PRELUDE

The chorale prelude, which is the third of the fugal forms, is less definite in outline than the concerto grosso and therefore more difficult to define with any degree of exactitude. It had its origin in the chorale tunes that were sung in Protestant churches after the time of Luther. Composers attached to the church exercised their ingenuity in making elaborate settings of these simple melodies. They are, in a sense, variations on a hymn tune, and I shall mention three of the best known types of treatment of these choral tunes.

The simplest method consists of keeping the given melody intact, while making the accompanying harmonies more interesting, either by increasing the harmonic complexity or by making the accompanying voices more intricately polyphonic. A second type embroiders upon the theme itself, lending the barest melodic outline an unsuspected grace and floridity. The third, and most involved, type is a kind of fugue woven around the tune of the chorale. For example, some fragment of the chorale tune may serve as fugue subject. An exposition of a fugue is written just as if there were to be no chorale; and then without warning, while the fugue continues along placidly, above or beneath it may be heard the long-drawn-out notes of the chorale.

Some of Bach's finest creations were written in one or another of these forms of chorale prelude. His *Orgelb uchlein* is a collection of short chorale preludes containing an inexhaustible wealth of musical riches, which no music lover can afford to ignore. Deeply moving from an expressive standpoint, they are nevertheless marvels of technical ingenuity—a magistral illustration of the welding of thought and emotion.

MOTETS AND MADRIGALS

The fourth and last of the fugal forms is that of motets and madrigals. I hasten to add that a motet or madrigal is not a form, properly speaking; but since they will be listened to with increasing frequency and definitely belong with the contrapuntal forms, their proper place is here. One cannot generalize as to their form, because they are choral compositions, sung without accompaniment and dependent on their words in each individual instance for their formal outline.

Motets and madrigals were written in profusion during the fifteenth, sixteenth, and seventeenth centuries. The difference between the two is that the motet is a short vocal composition on sacred words, whereas the madrigal is a similar composition on secular words. The madrigal is generally less severe in character. Both are typical vocal fugal forms of the era before the advent of Bach and his contemporaries.

From the listener's standpoint, it is important to distinguish the texture of motet or madrigal. Here, again, no rule prevails; motets and madrigals may be either fugal or chordal in style or a combination of both. I fail to see how these vocal forms may be heard intelligently without an elementary idea as to their different textures. In the motet or madrigal of fugal or contrapuntal texture, the fact that the separate melodic voices are attached to words will be found especially helpful in aiding the listener to hear the counterpoint more easily than in the purely instrumental forms.

The Renaissance period is crowded with masters who used these vocal forms. Palestrina in Italy, Or-

Fugal Form

lando di Lasso in the Netherlands, Vittoria in Spain; Byrd, Wilbye, Morley, and Gibbons in England are some of the outstanding names in one of the most remarkable eras in music. The unfamiliarity of most of our concertgoers with this extraordinary epoch is indicative of the comparatively narrow musical interests of our time.

13

Fundamental Forms

IV · SONATA FORM

Sonata as a Whole; Sonata Form Proper;
The Symphony

THE sonata form, for the present-day listener, has something of the same significance that the fugal forms had for listeners of the first part of the eighteenth century. For it is not too much to say that, since that time, the basic form of almost every extended piece of music has been related in some way to the sonata. The vitality of the form is astonishing. It is just as much alive today as it was during the period of its first development. The logic of the form as it was practiced in the early days, plus its malleability in the hands of later composers, accounts, no doubt, for its continuous hold on the imagination of musical creators for the past 150 years or more.

Of course, it must not be forgotten that when we speak of sonata form we are not discussing only the form to be found in pieces that are called sonatas, for the meaning of the term is much more widespread than that. Every symphony, for example, is a sonata for orchestra; every string quartet is a sonata for four strings; every concerto a sonata for a solo instrument and orchestra. Most overtures, also, are in the form of the first movement of a sonata. The usage of the term sonata itself is generally confined to compositions for a solo instrument, with or without piano accompaniment; but, as may easily be seen, that is not nearly broad enough to include the varied applications of what is, in fact, sonata form to different mediums.

Fortunately for the lay listener, the sonata form, in any of its many manifestations, is, on the whole, more immediately accessible than some of the other forms we have been studying. That is because the problem it presents is not one of listening for detail in separate measures, as in the fugue, but of following the broad outlines of large sections. Also, the texture of the sonata, as a rule, is not nearly so contrapuntal as that of the fugue. As texture, it is much more all-inclusive—almost anything goes within the broad confines of the sonata form.

Before venturing farther, the reader should be warned against one other possible confusion regarding the use of the term "sonata form." It is applied, as a matter of fact, to two different things. In the first place, we speak of sonata form when we mean an entire work consisting of three or four movements. On the other hand, we also speak of sonata form when we refer to a specific type of structure in music generally found in the first, and often also the last, movement of an entire sonata. Therefore, you must keep in mind two things: (1) the sonata as a whole and (2) the sonata form proper, sometimes referred to as sonata allegro, or first-movement form, the sonata allegro referring to the fact that almost all first movements of sonatas are in allegro (or fast) tempo.

There is still another distinction that must be kept in mind. When you go to a concert and find listed on the program a sonata for violin and piano by Handel or Bach, do not listen for the form under discussion here. The word sonata was used at that time in contradistinction to the word cantata—sonata being something to be played, and cantata something to be sung. Otherwise it bears little or no relation to the later sonata of Mozart and Haydn's time.

The sonata as we think of it is said to be largely the creation of one of Bach's sons, Karl Philipp Emanuel Bach. He is credited with having been one of the first composers to experiment with the new form of sonata, the classic outlines of which were later definitely set by Haydn and Mozart. Beethoven put all his genius into broadening the sonata-form conceptions of his time; and he was followed by Schumann and Brahms, who also extended, in a lesser way, the significance of the formal mold. By now the treatment of the form is so free as to be almost unrecognizable in certain cases. Nevertheless, much of the outer shell and a good deal of the psychological implications of the form are intact, even today.

THE SONATA AS A WHOLE

Three of four separate movements comprise the sonata as a whole. There are examples of two-movement and, more recently, one-movement sonatas, but these are exceptional. The most obvious distinction between the movements is one of tempo: in the three-movement species, it is fast—slow—fast; and in the four-movement sonata, it is usually fast—slow—moderately fast—very fast.

People generally want to know what it is that makes these three or four movements belong together. No one has come forward with a completely satisfactory answer to that question. Custom and familiarity make them *seem* to belong together, but I have always suspected that one could substitute the Minuet of Haydn's 98th symphony for the Minuet in Haydn's 99th symphony without sensing a serious lack of coherence in either work. Particularly in these early examples of the sonata, the movements are linked together more from the need of balance and contrast and certain tonality relationships than from any intrinsic connection with each other. Later on, as we shall see in the so-called cyclic form of the sonata, composers did try to link their movements through thematic unity while retaining the general characteristics of the separate movements.

Now let us consider, for a moment, the form of each of the separate movements of the sonata as a whole. Our descriptions are to be taken as generally true, for there is almost no statement that can be made about sonata form that some specific exceptional instance does not contradict. As has already been said, the first movement of any sonata—and I use that word generically to denote symphonies and string quartets and the like—is always in sonata-allegro form. We shall be investigating that form thoroughly a few pages farther on.

The second movement is usually the slow movement, but there is no such thing as a slow-movement form. It may be written in one of several different molds. For example, it may be a theme and variation such as we have already studied. Or it may be a slow version of a rondo form—either a short or an extended rondo. It might be even more simple than that, relating itself to the ordinary three-part sectional form. More rarely, it bears close resemblance to the first-movement sonata form. The listener must be prepared for any one of these various forms when hearing the slow movement.

The third movement is usually a minuet or scherzo. In the earlier works of Haydn and Mozart, it is the minuet; in later times, the scherzo. In either case, it is the *A-B-A*, three-part form which was discussed under Sectional Forms. Sometimes the second and third movements are interchangeable—instead of finding the slow movement second and the scherzo third, the scherzo may be second and the slow movement third.

The fourth movement, or finale, as it is often called,

is almost always either in extended rondo form or in sonata-allegro form. Thus it is only the first movement of the sonata that presents an entirely new physiognomy for us.

One-movement sonatas are generally of two types: either they confine themselves to an extended treatment of first-movement form; or they attempt to include all four movements within the limits of a single movement. Two-movement sonatas are too unpredictable to be catalogued.

SONATA-ALLEGRO, OR FIRST-MOVEMENT, FORM

It is one of the more remarkable features of the sonata-allegro form that it may so easily be reduced to the ordinary tripartite formula: *A-B-A*. As far as its broadest outlines are concerned, it does not differ from the tiny section analyzed in the chapter on Musical Structure or from the various kinds of three-part form considered under Sectional Forms. But it must be remembered in this case that each of the sections of the *A-B-A* represent large divisions of music, each of them lasting as much as five or ten minutes in length.

The conventional explanation of sonata-allegro form is easily demonstrated. It explains, for the most part, the earlier and less complex forms of the sonata alle-

Sonata Form

gro. A simple diagram will show the general outlines of the form:

Exposition	Development	Recapitulation

A :‖	B	A

a	b	c	a b c	a	b	c
tonic	dominant	dominant	foreign keys	tonic	tonic	tonic

As may be seen, the *A-B-A* of the formula is, in this instance, named exposition-development-recapitulation. In the exposition section, the thematic material is exposed; in the development section, it is handled in new and unsuspected ways; in the recapitulation, it is heard again in its original setting.

The exposition section contains a first theme, a second theme, and a closing theme.* The character of the first theme is dramatic, or "masculine," and it is always in the tonic key; the character of the second theme is lyrical, or "feminine," and it is always in the dominant key; the closing theme is less important than either of these and is also in the dominant key. The development section is "free"; that is, it freely combines the material introduced in the exposition and sometimes adds new material of its own. In this section, the music moves into new and foreign keys. The recapitulation restates more or less literally what was

---

*This schematic description is meant to indicate nothing more than the conventional framework as usually outlined, textbook fashion.

found in the Exposition, except that all the themes are now in the tonic key.

So much for the bare outlines of the form. Now let us examine it more closely and see if we cannot generalize regarding the form in such a way as to make it more applicable to actual examples of all periods.

All sonata allegros, of whatever period, retain the tripartite form of exposition-development-recapitulation. The exposition contains a variety of musical elements. That is its essential nature, for there would be little or nothing to develop if that were not so. These varied elements are usually divided into a small *a*, a small *b*, and a small *c*, representing what used to be called the first, second, and closing themes. I say "used to be called" because recent analysts have become dissatisfied with the obvious disparity between this nomenclature and the evidence presented by the actual works themselves. It is difficult to generalize with any degree of finality as to exactly what goes into an exposition section. Still, one can safely say that themes *are* exposed, that these themes are contrasted in character and that they bring some sense of close at the end of the section. For the sake of convenience, there would be no objection to calling the small *a* the first theme, provided it were clearly understood that actually it may consist of a conglomeration of several

Sonata Form

themes or fragments of themes, usually of a strongly dramatic and affirmative quality. The same is true of the *b*, so-called second, theme, which again may actually be a series of one or more themes, but of a more lyrical and expressive nature. This juxtaposition of one group of themes denoting power and aggressiveness with another group which is relaxed and more song-like in quality is the essence of the exposition section and determines the character of the entire sonata-allegro form. In many of the early examples of the form, the ordering of the material into first and second themes is more strictly adhered to, whereas later on we can be sure only that two opposing elements will be present in the exposition, without being able to say in exactly what sequence they will appear.

The last theme, or themes, under the heading of small *c*, constitutes a closing sentence or sentences. Therefore it may be of any nature that leads to a sense of conclusion. This is important, because an audience should have a clear idea of where the end of the exposition occurs, if it is expected to follow the development intelligently. If you read notes, you can always mechanically find the end of the exposition in any of the classic sonatas or symphonies by looking for the double bar with repeat sign, indicating the formal repetition of the entire section. Interpreters nowadays use their discretion in the matter of repeating the exposition. So that part of the problem of listening to the first-movement form is to watch out for this possibility of repetition. More modern sonatas and symphonies do not indicate any repetition, so that even if you read notes the end of the section is not so easily found.

One other element is important in the exposition. You cannot very well go from one mood that is powerfully dramatic to another that is lyrically expressive without some sort of transition. This transition, or bridge section, as it is often called, may be short or fairly elaborate. But it must never be of equal significance thematically with elements *a* or *b*, for that could lead only to confusion. Composers, at such moments, fall back upon a kind of musical figuration, or passage work, which is important because of its functional significance rather than for its intrinsic musical interest. Watch out, then, for the bridge between *a* and *b* and the possibility of a second bridge between *b* and *c*.

It is the development section that gives the sonata allegro its special character. In no other form is there a special division reserved for the extension and development of musical material already introduced in a previous section. It is that feature of the sonata-allegro

Sonata Form

form that has so fascinated all composers—that opportunity for working freely with materials already announced. So you see that the sonata form, properly understood, is essentially a psychological and dramatic form. You cannot very well mix the two or more elements of the exposition without creating a sense of struggle or drama. It is the development section that challenges the imagination of every composer. One might go so far as to say that it is one of the main things that separates the composer from the layman. For anyone can whistle tunes. But you really have to be a composer, with a composer's craft and technique, in order to be able to write a really fine development of those tunes.

No rules govern the development section. The composer is entirely free as to types of development, as to the thematic material chosen for development; as to the introduction of new materials, if any; and as to the length of the section as a whole. One can only generalize about two factors: (1) that the development usually begins with a partial restatement of the first theme in order to remind the listener of the starting point; and (2) that during the course of the development the music modulates through a series of far-off keys which serve to prepare a sense of homecoming when the original tonality is finally reached at the beginning of

[187]

the recapitulation. These things vary considerably, of course, in accordance with whether you examine an early or late example of sonata-allegro form. For instance, the development section became much more elaborate, even as early as Beethoven's day, than it had been before his time. The modulatory scheme has been adhered to, even in recent times, when the classic tonic-dominant-dominant relationship of the first, second, and closing themes, respectively, has completely broken down. More and more the trend has been to attach added importance to the development section, as I have already pointed out, so that it has become the pivotal section of the sonata-allegro form, into which the composer pours every ounce of imagination and invention that he possesses.

The recapitulation is, as its name indicates, a repetition of the exposition. In the classical sonata-allegro, the repetition is generally exact; though even here the inclination is to omit nonessentials, leaving out material already sufficiently heard. In later times, the repetition became more and more free until it sometimes is a mere wraith of its former self. It is not very difficult to understand why this is so. The sonata-allegro had its origin in a period when composers were "classically" minded; that is, they began with a structure whose outlines were perfectly clear, and into it they

Sonata Form

put a music well controlled and of an objective emotional quality. There was no contradiction between the formal *A-B-A* outline and the nature of the musical content. But with the advent of the romantic era, music became much more dramatic and psychological. It was inevitable that the new romantic content should be difficult to contain within the framework of an essentially classical formal scheme. For it is only logical to say that if the composer states his material in the exposition, and if he then develops it in a highly dramatic and psychological fashion, he really should come to a different conclusion about it in the end. What sense does it make to go through all the turmoil and struggle of the development section if it is only to lead back to the same conclusions from which we started? That is why the tendency on the part of modern composers to shorten the recapitulation or to substitute a new conclusion seems justified.

One of the most extraordinary mistakes in music is the example supplied us by Scriabin, the Russian composer of amazing gifts, who died in 1915. The quality of his thematic material was truly individual, truly inspired. But Scriabin, who wrote ten piano sonatas, had the fantastic idea of attempting to put this really new body of feeling into the strait jacket of the old classical sonata form, recapitulation and all. Few modern composers make that error any longer. In fact, they sometimes go to the other extreme, giving so liberal an interpretation to the word sonata as to make it practically meaningless. So that nowadays, the listener must be prepared for almost any application of the term.

Two important extensions were added to the form while it was still in the early stages of development. An introductory section preceded the "allegro," and a coda was tacked on at the end. The introduction is almost always slow in tempo, a sure indication that the *A* section has not yet begun. It may consist of musical materials which are entirely independent of the allegro to follow; or it may be that a slow version of the main theme in *A* is given out to further the feeling of unity. The coda cannot be so definitely described. From Beethoven on, it has played a preponderant role in stretching the boundaries of the form. Its purpose is to create a sense of apotheosis—the material is seen for the last time and in a new light. Here, again, no rules govern the procedure. At times, the treatment is so extended as to make the coda a kind of second development section though always leading toward a sense of epilogue and conclusion.

This summary of sonata-allegro form can be of value to the reader only if it is applied in listening to definite works. I have chosen as one example, out of many, Beethoven's Waldstein *Sonata* for piano, Op. 53, an analysis of which will be found in Appendix III. To profit from an analysis of this kind, it is necessary to hear a work over and over again. My own experience has taught me that I know a work thoroughly only when I am able mentally to sing it over to myself, to recreate it in my own mind, as it were. There is no better way of truly appreciating the differences between a mere diagrammatic outline of a form and a contact with the kaleidoscopic changes of a living organism. It is like the difference between reading a description of the physiognomy of a human being and knowing a living man or woman.

THE SYMPHONY

The present-day status of the symphony is such that it is impossible to pass it by without further discussion, even though it does not constitute an independent form, different from the sonata. It is practically impossible to hear an orchestral program in the concert hall or on the air without being confronted with one or another of the symphonies of the regular repertoire. It should be remembered, however, that these present no specific problems other than those outlined above.

What to Listen for in Music

The symphony had its origin not in instrumental forms like the concerto grosso, as one might have expected, but in the overture of early Italian opera. The overture, or sinfonia, as it was called, as perfected by Alessandro Scarlatti consisted of three parts: fast-slow-fast, thus presaging the three movements of the classical symphony. The sinfonia, around 1750, became detached from the opera which gave it birth and led an independent life in the concert hall. Karl Nef, in his *Outline of the History of Music*, describes what happened. "After the theatre symphony had been transferred to the concert hall, the musical world was seized by a veritable mania to play symphonies. The composers never published less than half a dozen at a time. Many of them wrote a hundred and more; the sum total mounted to many thousands. Under these circumstances it would be idle to attempt to discover the man who founded the new style. Numerous composers collaborated in the new movement, in the earliest period Italians, Frenchmen, and Germans."*

The best orchestra of the day was maintained from 1743 to 1777 in Mannheim. Here the precursors of Haydn and Mozart originated many of the features of the later symphony, such as the orchestral crescendo

*Reprinted by permission from Karl Nef, *An Outline of the History of Music*, translated by Carl F. Pfatteicher, Columbia University Press, 1935.

and diminuendo and a greater flexibility in the orchestral fabric. The general texture was more homophonic, borrowing from the lighter, singing quality of operatic style, rather than the heavier contrapuntal manner of the concerto grosso.

It was on this foundation that Haydn gradually perfected symphonic style. We must not forget that some of his greatest achievements in this medium were created after the death of Mozart and after a long period of gestation and maturity. He left the symphony a rounded art form, capable of further development but not of greater perfection within the limits of his own style.

The way was paved for Beethoven's famous Nine. The symphony lost all connection with its operatic origins. The form was enlarged, the emotional scope broadened, the orchestra stamped and thundered in a completely new and unheard-of fashion. Beethoven singlehandedly created a colossus which he alone seemed able to control.

For the nineteenth century composers who followed him—Schumann and Mendelssohn—wrote a less titanic symphony. By the middle of the century, the symphony was in danger of losing its hegemony in the orchestral field. The "modernists" Liszt, Berlioz, and Wagner apparently considered the symphony "old hat" unless it was combined with some programmatic idea or incorporated in essence into the body of a music drama. It was "conservatives" like Brahms, Bruckner, and Tschaikovsky who defended what began to look very much like a lost cause.

One important innovation was introduced during this period as regards symphonic form, namely, the so-called cyclic form of the symphony. César Franck was especially fond of this device. It was an attempt to bind the different parts of the entire work by unifying the thematic materials. Sometimes a "motto" theme is heard at unexpected moments in different movements of the symphony, giving an impression of a single unifying thought. At other times—and this is more truly cyclic form—all thematic material in an entire symphony may be derived from only a few primal themes, which are completely metamorphosed as the work progresses, so that what was first given out as a sober introductory theme is transformed into the principal melody of the scherzo, and similarly in slow movement and finale.

If the cyclic form has not been adopted more widely, it is probably because it does not solve the need for musical logic within each separate movement. That is, the unification of all the thematic material is no more than a device, more or less interesting depending upon the ingenuity with which it is carried out by the composer, but the symphony itself must still be written! The same problems of form and substance must be grappled with, compared to which the derivation of all the material from a single source is only a detail. After Franck, his pupil and disciple Vincent d'Indy made use of cyclic form, and more recently Ernest Bloch has utilized it in more than one work.

Not so very long ago, the impression was current that modern composers had abandoned the form of the symphony. No doubt there was a lull in interest on the part of leading men of the first twenty years of the present century. Debussy, Ravel, Schoenberg, and Béla Bartók in their mature years did not write symphonies. But more recently that has changed. Symphonies have been written again, if we can judge by the works of Frenchmen like Milhaud and Honegger; Russians like Miaskovsky (with twenty-seven to his credit), Prokofieff and Shostakovitch; Englishmen like Bax, Vaughan Williams, and Walton; Americans like Harris, Sessions, and Piston. We should not forget the further fact that even during the period of its supposed decline, the symphonic form was being practiced by stalwarts such as Mahler and Sibelius. Perhaps it is indicative of a renewed interest in the form that only in the present day have their works begun to find a place in the regular repertoire of symphonic organizations.

Mahler and Sibelius have been more adventurous in their treatment of the form than some of the later men. Mahler wanted desperately to make the symphony *bigger* than it was. He enlarged the size of the orchestra to gargantuan proportions, increased the number of movements, introduced the choral body in the *Second* and *Eighth*, and in general took it upon himself to carry on the traditions of the Beethoven symphony. Mahler has been bitterly attacked as a poseur, as having been hopelessly misled in his pretensions. But if one can pick and choose among the separate movements of his nine symphonies, I for one am certain that his eventual position will be equivalent to that of Berlioz. At any rate, we can find the derivation of new contrapuntal textures and new orchestral colors in his work, without which the modern symphony would be inconceivable.

Sibelius has handled the form freely, especially in his *Fourth* and *Seventh* symphonies. The latter belongs with the rather rare species of one-movement symphonies. Much has been written of Sibelius' masterly development of symphonic form. But it is a question whether his departures from the usual norm have not been so great as to be almost disconnected from the nineteenth-century model. My own guess is that the *Seventh* is closer in form, despite its name, to the symphonic poem than it is to the symphony. At any rate, from the lay listener's point of view, it must be remembered that Sibelius' movements are not conventionally constructed and depend more on the gradual organic growth of one theme evolving into another rather than the contrast of one theme with another. At its best, the music seems to flower, often from unpromising beginnings.

If any generalizations may be made as to the handling of the form by more recent composers, one can safely say that the symphony as a collection of three or more separate movements is still as firmly established as ever. There is still nothing puny or casual about the form. It is still the form in which the composer tries to come to grips with big emotions. If any fundamental changes may be discerned, they are likely to be changes of the inner structural setup of an individual movement. In that restricted sense, the form is freer—the materials are introduced in a more relaxed way—the divisions into first, second, and closing groups are much less clear if they are present at all; no one can predict the nature of the development section or the extent of the recapitulation, if any. That's why the modern symphony is more difficult to listen to than the older, to us more fully digested, examples of the form.

Clearly, the symphony, and with it the sonata-allegro form, is not finished yet. Unless all signs are misleading, they both will have a healthy progeny.

14

Fundamental Forms

V · FREE FORMS

The Prelude; The Symphonic Poem

I N ORDER to have some conception of what a "free" form consists of, we have to know what a strict form is. In the previous four chapters, fundamental forms of the strict variety were summarized. We discovered that the mere description of the outer structural frame of a piece does not encompass the true inner form of that piece; that all formal molds are freely used by the composer, so that he may be said to be both dependent and independent of them at the same time.

All forms that do not have as point of reference one of the usual formal molds are technically "free" forms. We also put the word "free" in quotation marks because, properly speaking, there is no such thing as an absolutely free musical form. No matter how free a piece may be, it must always make sense as form. That much is obvious; it is true of any art, and especially true of music where it is so easy to lose the feeling of coherence. Therefore, even in so-called free forms, some basic formal plan will certainly be present, though it may be unrelated to any of the normal formal molds that we have considered up to now.

Certain types of composition seem to fall more naturally than others into forms that are "free." Vocal works, for example, because of the necessity for following the words, often fall into that category. The church Mass, for instance, despite the fact that the general outlines of its separate parts are predetermined, has almost limitless possibilities for variety. One composer may write a very short opening Kyrie, whereas another will stretch it out to last for fifteen minutes. In general, vocal compositions are "freer" in form than instrumental works.

Among instrumental pieces, piano and orchestral

Free Forms

works are more likely to be in "free" forms than chamber music. This may have come about because "free" forms are so often used in music in connection with extramusical ideas, and chamber music almost always fits into the category of so-called "absolute music." It is only natural that if a composer starts with an extramusical idea, he will probably find the stereotyped patterns of the usual forms too constricting for his purposes. Many recent examples of "free" form may be credited to that source.

It is obviously impossible to make generalizations about "free" forms. Nevertheless, it is safe to say that we are likely to meet them in one of two types of composition: the prelude and the symphonic, or tone, poem.

The prelude is a very loose term for a large variety of pieces, generally written for piano. As a title, it may mean almost anything from a quiet, melancholy piece to a long and showy, virtuoso piece. But as form it will generally be found to belong in the "free" category. Prelude is a generic name for any piece of not too specific formal structure. Many other pieces with different names belong in the same category—pieces that are called fantasy, elegy, impromptu, capriccio, aria, étude, and so forth. Pieces such as these may be in strict *A-B-A* form, or they may be "freely" treated.

What to Listen for in Music

The listener, therefore, must be on the alert if he expects to follow the composer's structural idea.

Bach wrote a good many preludes (very often followed by a balancing fugue) many of which are in "free" form. It was these that Busoni pointed to as an example of the path that he thought music should take. Bach achieved a unity of design in these "free" preludes either by adopting a pattern of well-defined character or by a clear progression of chordal harmonies which lead one from the beginning of a piece to the end without utilizing any repetition of thematic materials. Often, both methods are combined. By these means Bach engenders a feeling of free fantasy and a bold freedom of design that would be impossible to achieve within a strict form. When one hears them, the conviction grows that Busoni was quite right in saying that the future problems of handling form in music are bound up with this Bach-like freedom in form.

An excellent illustration is the B flat major Prelude from Bach's *Well Tempered Clavichord*, Book I. Here there can be no question of themes and their being built up by sections. The music begins with this pattern (see opposite page).

By the time the halfway mark has been reached, Bach abandons his pattern for a series of full-sounding chords, interspersed with roulades and scale passages.

Only in the penultimate measure is there a reference to the pattern of the beginning, and even then there is no actual repetition of notes but merely one of pattern. The only outward sign of a unifying principle in a piece of this kind is the skeletal chordal frame. Other illustrations of a much grander kind are to be found in

[203]

Bach's *Fantasies*, for instance in the *Chromatic Fantasy and Fugue* or the famous G minor organ *Fantasy and Fugue*. Particularly in his big organ works, Bach creates an extraordinary sense of magnificence through utilization of this freer type of structure.

For the larger part of the nineteenth century, composers wrote in forms that are easily identified. This was due, no doubt, to the considerable degree of variety that could be achieved within the limits of three-part, or sonata-allegro, form. But even later in the century, with the advent of Richard Strauss, who certainly was preoccupied with the problems of "free" forms in his large orchestral works, the emphasis is still on the statement of themes and their full development.

Much of the revival of interest in true "free" forms during the present century is attributable, I believe, to Debussy's influence. He had very little precedent in the music of his time for the highly individual fashion in which he worked in short forms. Without depending upon any known models, he composed twenty-four *Preludes* for piano, each one of which has its own formal character. Each new *Prelude* meant inventing a new form, for the writing of one did not help in the creation of the next. No wonder his output was comparatively small.

Just as in the case of the pattern design of Bach,

Free Forms

Debussy sometimes makes use of a tiny figure, or motif, as an aid in binding a piece together. Take, for example, the piano prelude called *Footsteps in the Snow* (*Des pas sur la neige*). Here the tiny motif is consistently retained as background throughout the piece. It is a combination of a single rhythm which melodically moves a step upward each time, thus:*

Above that mysteriously evocative figure, a typically Debussian melody, wraithlike and fragmentary, is heard. Note that the melody is never repeated; instead

*Permission of reprint granted by Durand & Cie, Paris, and Elkan-Vogel Company, Inc., Philadelphia, copyright owners.

it seems gradually to come to life of its own accord, through a series of hesitations and secret impulses until, delicately but surely, a sense of completion is obtained. The piece certainly is unified, but the means for unification are quite different from those used by Debussy's forerunners.

Since Debussy's time, form has tended toward greater and greater freedom, until it now presents serious obstacles for the lay listener. Two things make music easy to listen to: a melody that is straightforward and plenty of repetition. New music often contains rather recondite melodies and avoids repetition. An opposite tendency has asserted itself—the urge toward condensation. One can see that tendency most clearly in the *Piano Pieces*, Op. 19, of Arnold Schoenberg, a work of his middle period (no recording available). In each of these little piano pieces, the intensity of emotion is so great that repetition would be unthinkable. Sometimes there is no theme to speak of—in one piece a tiny rhythm, in another a single chord is enough to hold the listener. When a melody is present, neither is it easy to grasp, nor does it ever stop to go over ground already covered. It isn't surprising therefore, that audiences find Schoenberg hard to take. In general, I should say that half the difficulty music lovers find in understanding so-called modern music comes from a lack of comprehension of the way in which the music is put together.

SYMPHONIC POEM

One of the reasons for our present freedom of form may very well be the creation of the symphonic poem. The symphonic, or tone, poem brings up the question of program music which must be elucidated first.

The reader should clearly distinguish in his own mind the difference between program music, which is music connected in some way with a story or poetic idea, and so-called "absolute" music, which has no extramusical connotations. To use music as a means of describing something outside itself is a perfectly natural, almost childlike idea. It is a rather old idea, as a matter of fact, for even composers of the seventeenth century had a penchant for describing things musically. Battles were favorite themes; also the imitation of animals was in high favor even before the flowering of instrumental music. Kuhnau, a predecessor of Bach and Handel, has made himself justly famous with his *Bible Sonatas*, in which biblical stories, such as the slaying of Goliath by David, are "realistically" portrayed in the music. Jannequin's remarkable *Chant des oiseaux* will give an excellent illustration of what a composer of the sixteenth century could do in the way of imitating the sounds of birds by means of a chorus of human beings. *Women's Cackle* was another subject he essayed. So you see the idea is not a new one.

But it wasn't until the nineteenth century that composers were really able to describe things well. Music became less and less naïve. Nowadays if you wish to reenact a battle musically, given a modern orchestra, the chances are that you can probably create a pretty unpleasantly realistic picture. The nineteenth century, in other words, developed the means for a more exact depiction in musical terms of extramusical events. Perhaps the development of opera also was responsible for interesting composers in the descriptive powers of music. Nor must we forget the influence of the romantic movement. It wasn't enough for a romantic composer to write a sad piece; he wanted you to know who it was that felt sad and the particular circumstances of his sadness. That is why Tschaikovsky was not satisfied to write an untitled overture with a beautiful second theme but called it *Romeo and Juliet*, thereby labeling the theme as the "Romeo's-love-for-Juliet" motif.

Beethoven himself, as witness the *Pastoral Symphony*, was attracted by the idea of describing out-

Free Forms

ward events in musical terms. His was one of the first examples of descriptive orchestral music. What Beethoven began in his *Sixth Symphony*, as an exceptional work, Berlioz made the basis for an entire career. The *Fantastic Symphony* is an amazing example of the progress composers had made in the nineteenth century in the ability to describe graphically not only pastoral or warlike scenes but any event or idea that they chose to depict.

Speaking generally, there are two kinds of descriptive music. The first comes under the heading of literal description. A composer wishes to recreate the sound of bells in the night. He therefore writes certain chords, for orchestra or piano or whatever medium he is using, which actually sound like bells in the night. Something real is being imitated realistically. A famous example of that kind of description in music is the passage in one of Strauss's tone poems where he imitates the bleating of sheep. The music has no other *raison d'être* than mere imitation at that point.

The other type of descriptive music is less literal and more poetic. No attempt is made to describe a particular scene or event; nevertheless some outward circumstance arouses certain emotions in the composer which he wishes to communicate to the listener. It may be clouds or the sea or a country fair or an airplane. But the point is that instead of literal imitation, one gets a musicopoetic transcription of the phenomenon as reflected in the composer's mind. That constitutes a higher form of program music. The bleating of sheep will always sound like the bleating of sheep, but a cloud portrayed in music allows the imagination more freedom.

One principle must be kept firmly in mind: No matter how programmatic or descriptive music may be, it must always exist in terms of music alone. Never allow a composer to justify his piece to you because of the story content. It is not sufficient to close a piece slowly because the heroine meets an untimely end. That slow end must also be justified by the musical content. In short, story interest can never take the place of musical interest; nor can it be made an excuse for musical procedure. The music must be able to stand on its own feet, so that a person hearing it with no knowledge of the story would not have his enjoyment curtailed in any way. In other words, the story must never be more than an added attraction. *Romeo and Juliet* is one of Tschaikovsky's best pieces even if you don't know the title. The first theme is dramatic and exciting and well knit. If you happen to be aware that it symbolizes the fight between the rival houses of Montague and Capulet, the theme

Free Forms

may seem more pertinent to you; but at the same time it undoubtedly limits its imaginative appeal. That is the danger that all programmatic music runs. Possibly because of it, composers nowadays do not write nearly so much program music as was customary at the end of the past century.

Surprisingly enough, a considerable amount of program music is written in one or another of the fundamental forms. One would have expected that since the composer was describing something, the form would necessarily be free. That is often not the case. In the beginning, especially, the hold of absolute music and its formal molds was too strong to be ignored. Thus Beethoven's *Pastoral Symphony* is a symphony first and a pastoral symphony only in a secondary sense. Likewise, the passionate drama of *Romeo* fits with surprising ease into the regular sonata-allegro form with an introduction, first and second theme, development, and recapitulation. It wasn't until Strauss and Debussy that composers had the courage to abandon stricter forms for the sake of greater fidelity to their programmatic intentions. The beginning of that greater freedom was, of course, the creation of the symphonic poem, one of the few new forms in the nineteenth century.

Liszt is generally credited with having originated

the symphonic poem. He wrote thirteen of them himself, some of which are still performed. Liszt realized that a poetic idea, if it was to be properly expressed, could not be confined to the limits of the stricter forms, even as applied by Berlioz in his programmatic symphonies. The one-movement symphonic poem, with an introductory explanation printed in the published score, was his solution. Liszt's example was followed by other composers, notably Saint-Saëns, César Franck, Paul Dukas, Tschaikovsky, Smetana, Balakireff, and a host of lesser men. Not all their tone poems are in "free" forms. But the principle had been established.

Richard Strauss, between 1890 and 1900, wrote a series of symphonic poems which astonished the musical world by their freedom and daring. They were the logical heirs of Liszt's idea but on a much grander and more pretentious plane. The earlier symphonic poem was analogous with a single movement of a symphony, but the Straussian tone poem is more the equivalent of the full-sized symphony. Despite obvious weaknesses, which may eventually affect their present seemingly solid position in the symphonic repertoire, they are remarkable achievements. As pictorial representation they have few rivals, and as treatment of

Free Forms

forms that were free they were the first of their kind. Even when they lean on one of the stricter forms such as the rondo (*Till Eulenspiegel*) or the variation (*Don Quixote*)), the handling of the material is so unconventional as to constitute what is practically a "free" form. In *Ein Heldenleben* (*A Hero's Life*) or *Also sprach Zarathustra*, where the form may be said to be sectionally built, the mere size is so big as to make the composition dangerously top-heavy. It is a question whether the human mind can really relate the separate moments of a free form that lasts more than forty minutes without pause. That, at any rate, is what Strauss asks us to do. To grasp adequately the formal contours of a Strauss tone poem would take more explaining than is possible within the limits of this book.

To bring the programmatic idea up to date is a very simple matter. All that is necessary is to describe in musical terms some typically modern phenomenon such as an industrial plant or a streamlined speedboat. By so doing it is easy enough to give the old idea a specious air of modernity. As I have already said, recent composers have not written much program music. Nevertheless, there have been exceptions. Arthur Honegger came in for a considerable amount of notoriety because of his short orchestral piece called *Pacific*

What to Listen for in Music

2–3–1. The title refers to a specific type of locomotive which is known by that name in Europe. Honegger took advantage of the fact that there is a certain analogy between the slow starting of a train, its gradual pickup of speed, its rush through space, and the slowing down to a full stop—and music. He manages very well to give the listener an impression of the hissing of steam and the chug-chug of the mechanism and, at the same time, to write a piece solidly constructed of melodies and harmonies like any other piece. *Pacific 2–3–1* is an excellent example of modern program music; if it is not a great piece of music, it is because of the poor quality of some of the melodic material rather than the treatment of the programmatic idea itself.

Program music, in this literal sense, is apparently on the wane. Honegger wrote a second programmatic piece called *Rugby;* Mossolov wrote his *Iron Foundry;* other composers have used prize fights, skating rinks, radio stations, Ford factories, five and ten cent stores as material for musical description. But the trend away from impressionist music on the one hand and the urge toward neoclassicism on the other has left program music with comparatively few adherents. Composers nowadays, or most of them, prefer not to mix their categories; either they write straight theatrical

Free Forms

works or they write absolute music. But no one can prophesy when program music may develop a recrudescence of interest. New electrical instruments, when they are sufficiently perfected, will undoubtedly open up brand-new possibilities for the imitative powers of music.

15

Opera and Music Drama

U P TO now, the question of listening more intelligently has been considered solely in relation to
music that comes under the heading of concert music.
Strange as it may seem, music that is an end in itself,
having no connection with any extramusical idea, is
not the natural phenomenon that it seems to be. Music did not begin as concert music, certainly. It was
only after century-long historical developments that

music, listened to for its own sake, was able to seem self-sufficient.

Theatrical music, on the other hand, is, by comparison, a perfectly natural thing. Its origins go as far back as the primitive ritual music of a savage tribe or the religious chant of a sacred play in the Middle Ages. Even today, music written to accompany a play, film, or ballet seems self-explanatory. The only form of theatrical music that is at all controversial, and therefore in need of some explaining, is the operatic form.

Opera in our own day is an art form with a somewhat tarnished reputation. I speak, naturally, of the opinion of the musical "elite." That wasn't always true. There was a time when opera was thought of as a more advanced form than any other. But until quite recently, it was customary among the elite to speak of the operatic form with a certain amount of condescension.

There were several reasons for the disrepute into which opera fell. Among the first of these was the fact that opera bore the "taint" of Wagner about it. For at least thirty years after his death, the entire musical world made heroic efforts to throw off the terrific impact of Wagner. That is no reflection on his music. It simply means that each new generation must create its own music; and it was a very difficult thing to do, particularly in the opera house, immediately after Wagner had lived.

Moreover, quite aside from Wagnerian music drama, it might truthfully be said that the public that flocked to hear opera did the form little credit. On the one hand, it became associated with what was sometimes called a "barber public"—musical groundlings for whom the real art of music was assumed to be a closed book. On the other hand, there was the "society public," turning the opera into a fashionable playground, with an eye only for its circus aspect.

Moreover, the repertoire currently performed was made up for the most part of old "chestnuts," outmoded show pieces that were fit only to strike awe in the mind of a movie magnate. How could one possibly think of injecting into this situation a new opera written in the more up-to-date manner of the 1920's, despite the fact that this new, revolutionary music was already invading the concert halls? To the musical elite, all music of serious pretentions seemed to be automatically ruled out of the opera house. If by lucky chance a new work did reach the operatic stage, it was more than likely to be found too esoteric for the audience, if it hadn't previously been annihilated by the artificialities of the conventional opera production.

Those are some of the reasons for the low estimate

Opera and Music Drama

of the opera as a form in the opinion of the people who look upon music seriously. But around 1924 a renewal of interest in opera began, which had its origin in Germany. Every small town in Germany has an opera house. There were said to be, around that time, at least ten first-class and twenty second-class operatic stages that functioned most of the year round. We must not forget that in Germany the opera takes the place of our musical comedy, movie, and theater combined. Every good citizen owns his weekly subscription to the opera, so that there was almost a social obligation for opera to renew itself as a form. Moreover, publishers of music did much to encourage the writing of new operatic works. A really successful opera brought a large financial return to both authors and publishers. There was then plenty of incentive for composers to write operas and publishers to print them, plus the added advantage of a postwar audience interested in experiencing new operatic ventures off the conventional path. Before long, interest spread to other countries, and even our own Metropolitan half-heartedly paid its respects to new opera by an occasional performance of a representative modern work.

If the reader is to be convinced that the life newly imbued in opera has some justification, he must have some understanding of opera as a form. I feel sure that many of my readers are convinced that opera is a dull form and do not ever want to go to an operatic performance if they can possibly avoid it. Let us see what can be said to break down that prejudice.

The first point to be made, and one that cannot be too strongly emphasized, is that opera is bound from head to foot by convention. Of course, opera is not the only form of art that is so bound. The theater, for example, pretends that the fourth wall of a room is there and that we, in some miraculous way, look on while real life is being enacted. Children who visit the theater for the first time imagine that everything that occurs there is really happening; but we grownups have no trouble in accepting the convention of the stage as real, though we very well know that the actors are only making believe. The point is that opera has its conventions, too—and still greater ones than the theater. It is important for you to realize to what an extent you accept convention in the theater if you are to be less reluctant to accept the still greater one of the opera house.

In a sense, an opera is simply a drama sung instead of a drama spoken. That is the first of the conventions and completely at variance with reality. Even so, the drama is not sung continuously (until Wagner's time, at any rate) but, instead, is broken up into regularly contrasted, set musical pieces—which removes it one step farther from any connection with the reality that it is supposedly depicting. Moreover, the story that is being told is often of a fatuity that can hardly be exaggerated. Nothing sensible ever seems to take place on an operatic stage. Nor does the acting of opera singers conspire to aid in making the libretto—as the book of an opera is called—any the less fatuous.

Finally, there is the matter of the recitative—that part of an opera which is neither spoken nor sung but rather is half sung—telling the story part (especially in old operas), without any attempt at stimulating musical interest. When an opera is sung in a language unfamiliar to the listener, as most operas are in English-speaking countries, these recitative sections can be of surpassing boredom. These facts go to prove that the opera is not a realistic form of art; and one must not demand that it be realistic. As a matter of fact, no one is more tiresome than the person who can understand only realism in art. It shows a rather low artistic mentality never to believe anything you see unless it appears to be real. One must be willing to allow that symbolic things also mirror realities and sometimes provide greater esthetic pleasure than the merely realistic. The opera house is a good place in which to find these more symbolic pleasures. In short, what I have been trying to convey is that in order to enjoy what goes on in the opera house you must begin by accepting its conventions.

It is surprising that some people still consider opera a dead form. What makes it so different from any of the other forms of music is its all-inclusiveness. It contains within itself almost every musical medium: the symphony orchestra, the solo voice, the vocal ensemble, the chorus. The character of the music may be either serious or light—and both in the same work. Opera may contain music of a symphonic, or "absolute," nature, or it may be purely descriptive and programmatic. An opera also contains ballet, pantomime, and drama. It passes easily from one to the other. In other words, it is almost impossible to imagine any type of musical or theatrical art that would not be at home in an opera house.

But added to that is the spectacular display which only the opera can give in its own way. It is theater on a grand scale—crowds of people on the stage; magnificence of lights, costumes, and scenery. A composer who isn't attracted by such a medium has very little theatricalism in his soul. Most creators apparently have their share, for opera has fascinated some of the world's finest composers.

The problem of writing an opera is the combination

of all these disparate elements to form an artistic whole. It is anything but an easy problem. As a matter of fact, it is practically impossible to choose any one opera and say: "That's the perfect opera! There is the solution of the form that everyone must follow." In a sense, the problem is insoluble, for it is almost impossible to equalize and balance the different elements in an opera in such a way as to achieve a completely satisfying whole. The result has been, practically speaking, that composers have tended to emphasize one element at the expense of another.

That particularly applies to the words of an opera, as the first of the elements with which the composer works. Operatic composers have in practice done one of two things: Either they have given the words a preponderant role, using the music only to serve the drama; or they have frankly sacrificed the words, using them merely as a peg on which to hang their music. So that the entire problem of opera may be reduced to the diametrical pull of words on the one hand and music on the other. It is instructive to look at the history of opera from this standpoint and note the way in which composers solved this problem, each one for himself.

The year 1600 provides a convenient starting point, for it was thereabouts that operatic history began. It was the result—or so the historian tells us—of the meetings of certain composers and poets at the palace of one Count Bardi in Florence. Remember that serious art music up to that time had been almost entirely choral and of a highly contrapuntal and involved nature. In fact, music had become so contrapuntal, so complex, that it was well-nigh impossible to understand a word of what the singers were saying. The "new music" was going to change all that. Note immediately two fundamental qualities of opera at its very inception. First, the emphasis on stressing the words, making the music tell a story. Second, the "high-society" aspect of opera from the very start. (It was forty years before the first public opera house was opened in Venice.)

The ostensible purpose of the men who met at Count Bardi's was the revival of Greek drama. They wished to attempt the recreation of what they thought went on in the Greek theater. Of course, what they accomplished was a completely different thing—the creation of a new form, which was destined to fire the imagination of artists and audiences for generations to come.

The first of the great opera composers was the Italian, Claudio Monteverdi. Unfortunately, his works are rarely given nowadays and would strike our present-day opera lovers as little more than museum pieces if they were performed. From our vantage point, Monteverdi's style is limited in resource—it consists for the most part of what we should call recitative. Nowadays we think of the recitative as of very minor interest in an opera, and we wait always for the aria which follows it to arouse us. In our sense, Monteverdi's operas are innocent of arias, so that they seem to be nothing but one long recitative, with an occasional orchestral interlude. But what is so very extraordinary about the recitative in Monteverdi is its quality. It rings absolutely true; it is amazingly felt. Despite the fact that he comes at almost the very beginning of the new form, no one after Monteverdi was able to put words to music so simply, so movingly, so convincingly. In listening to Monteverdi, it is necessary to understand the meaning of the words, since he puts so much emphasis upon them. That is also true much later in operatic history when certain composers returned to the Monteverdian ideal of opera.

The new art form, which had begun so auspiciously, spread gradually to other countries outside Italy. It went first from Venice to Vienna and from Vienna to Paris, London, and Hamburg. Those were the big operatic centers in the 1700's. By that time, the opera had veered away from the Monteverdi prototype. The

[225]

words became less and less important, while all emphasis was placed upon the musical side of the opera. The newer form condensed the emotion aroused by the action into what we now think of as arias; and these arias were connected by recitative passages. But these sections are not to be confused with the Monteverdi species of recitative; they were ordinary, workaday recitatives designed merely for the purpose of telling the story as quickly as possible so that the next aria might be reached. The result was a form of opera that consisted of a collection of arias interspersed with recitative. There was no attempt at picturizing in the music events that happened on the stage. That was to come later.

The great opera composer of the seventeenth century was Alessandro Scarlatti, the father of the clavecin composer Domenico, whose works were commented upon in the discussion of two-part form. The model of opera that the elder Scarlatti developed we now connect with the later operas of Handel. In this type of opera, the story is of little import; the drama is static, and the action negligible. All interest is centered on the singer and the vocal part, and opera justifies itself only in terms of its musical appeal. It proved to be a dangerous development, for it wasn't long before the natural desire of singers to hold the center of the stage led to serious abuses which are still by no means entirely eradicated. The rivalry of singers led to the addition of all kinds of roulades and extra furbishings to the melodic line for the sole purpose of demonstrating the prowess of the particular interpreter in question.

What followed was inevitable. Since opera had become so highly formalized and unnatural an art form, someone was bound to come forward as a reformer. The history of opera is sprinkled with reformers. Someone is always trying to make opera more real than it was in the period just before him. The champion of reform who wished to correct the abuses of the Handelian opera was, of course, Christoph Willibald von Gluck.

Gluck himself had written a great many operas in the conventional Italian style of his day before he assumed the role of reformer, so that he knew whereof he spoke when he said that opera was in need of purification. Gluck tried above all to rationalize opera—to have it make more sense. In the older opera, the singer was supreme, and the music served the singer; Gluck made the dramatic idea supreme and wrote music that served the purposes of the text. Each act was to be an entity in itself, not a nondescript collection of more or less effective arias. It was to be balanced and

[227]

contrasted, with a flow and continuity that would give it coherence as an art form. The ballet, for example, was not to be a mere divertissement introduced for its own sake but an integral part of the dramatic idea of the work.

Gluck's ideas as to operatic reform were sound. Moreover, he was able to incorporate them into actual works. *Orpheus and Eurydice, Armide, Alceste* are the names of some of his most successful achievements. In these operas, he created a massive, stolid kind of music which fitted very well the grandiose subject matter of many of his works. And concomitant with the monumental impression is one of extraordinary calm, a species of calm beauty which is unique in music and utterly removed from the frivolities of the operatic medium of his day. Gluck's works are not to be classed as museum pieces; they are the first operas of which it may be said that time has not impaired their effectiveness.

That is not to say that Gluck was entirely successful in his reform. His operas are undoubtedly more rational than those which preceded him, but much was left to be accomplished by later men. His reform was only a relative one; in many instances, he merely substituted his own conventions for those that were current before him. But he was, nevertheless, a genius of the first rank, and he did succeed in setting up an ideal of opera that showed the way to future reformers.

Mozart, the next great name in operatic history, was not by nature a reformer. What we expect to find in Mozart is perfection in whatever medium he chose to work. Mozart's operas are no exception, for they embody more resourcefulness than can be found in any other opera up to his time. The *Magic Flute* is sometimes spoken of as the most perfect opera ever written. Its subject matter lends itself very well to operatic treatment because of its nonrealistic nature. It is both serious and comic, combining a wealth of musical imagination with a popular style accessible to all.

One contribution that Mozart did make to the form was the operatic finale. This is an effect possible only in opera—that final scene of an act when all the principals sing at the same time, each one singing about something else, only to conclude with a resounding fortissimo to the delight of everyone concerned. Mozart accomplished this typically musical trick in so definitive and perfect a way that all who used it after him—as who has not?—were indebted to him. It appears to be a fundamental effect in operatic writing, since it is just as much alive today as it was in Mozart's time.

Mozart was also in advance of his time in one other

respect. He was the first great composer to write a comedy set in the German language. *The Abduction from the Seraglio*, produced in 1782, is the first milestone in the path that leads directly to the future German opera. It set the style for a long list of followers, among whom may be counted the Wagner of the *Meistersinger*.

Richard Wagner was the next great reformer in opera. It was his purpose, as it had been Gluck's, to rationalize operatic form. He visualized the form as a union of all the arts—to include poetry, the drama, music, and the arts of the stage—everything connected with the spectacular opera outlined in the beginning of this chapter. He wished to give a new dignity to the operatic form by naming it music drama. Music drama was to be different from opera in two important respects: In the first place, the set musical number was to be done away with in favor of a continuous musical flow which followed an uninterrupted course from the beginning of an act to its conclusion. The opera of the separate aria connected by recitative was abandoned for the sake of greater realism in the dramatic form. Secondly, the famous conception of the leitmotif was introduced. Through associating a particular musical phrase, or motif, with each character or idea in the music drama, a greater cohesion of musical elements was to be assured.

But most significant in the Wagnerian music drama is the role assigned the orchestra. I had a most pronounced impression of that fact at the Metropolitan one winter on hearing Massenet's *Manon* one night and Wagner's *Die Walküre* the next. With the Frenchman's work one never gave the orchestra any special attention. It played a part not unlike that of a group of theater musicians in a pit; but as soon as Wagner's orchestra sounded, one had the impression that the entire Philharmonic Symphony had moved into the Metropolitan. Wagner brought the symphony orchestra to the opera house, so that the principal interest is often not on the stage but in the orchestra pit. The singers often must be listened to only in a secondary way, while the primary attention is placed on what the orchestra is "saying." Wagner was by nature a symphonist who applied his symphonic gifts to the form of the opera.

The question remains: "Did Wagner achieve reality in the opera house?" The answer must be "No." He achieved it no more than Gluck had. Once again, different conventions were substituted for those current in Wagner's time. Also, we may ask with justice: "Did he achieve the equality of all the arts which he never tired of proclaiming?" There, again, the answer is "No." The honest listener who witnesses a Wagnerian performance is bound to come away with an impression that is primarily a musical, not a dramatic, one. Imagine a Wagner libretto set to different music— none would evince the slightest interest in it. It is only because the music is so extraordinary that Wagner maintains his hold on the public. It is the music that is supreme; by comparison with it, all the other elements of the music drama are weak. Professor Edward Dent of Cambridge has exactly expressed my sentiments in relation to the extramusical considerations of Wagnerian drama. He has said: "A great deal of nonsense has been written, some indeed by Wagner himself, about the philosophical and moral significance of his operas." The final test of music drama, as of opera, must be the opera house itself. It is only the overpowering command of musical resources represented by Wagner's work that makes it bearable in the opera house.

Only two or three contemporaries were able to compete with Wagner on his own ground. Verdi was the principal of these. Like Gluck, he wrote a large number of conventional Italian operas, which were wildly acclaimed by the public but found little favor with the nineteenth-century admirers of music drama. But there has been a tendency in recent years on the part of the cognoscenti to reestimate the contribution made by Verdi. Somewhat chastened, not to say bored, by the static and "philosophical" music-drama stage, they are now in a position better to appreciate the virtuoso theatrical gifts of a man like Verdi. His operas were no doubt too traditional, too facile, and at times even too vulgar; but they *moved*. Verdi was a born man of the theater—the sheer effectiveness of works like *Aïda*, *Rigoletto*, *Traviata* assure them a permanent place in the operatic repertoire.

Verdi himself was somewhat influenced by the example of Wagner in the composition of his last two works, *Otello* and *Falstaff*, both written when the composer was past seventy. He put aside the separate operatic aria, used the orchestra in a more sophisticated manner, concentrated more directly on the dramatic implications of the plot. But he did not relinquish his instinctive feeling for the stage. That is why these two works—amazing examples of the powers of an old man—are on the whole better models for the edification of the young opera composer than the more theoretical music drama of Wagner.

Moussorgsky and Bizet were both able to create operas that are worthy of comparison with the best of Verdi or Wagner. Of the two, the Russian's operas

[233]

have had the more fruitful progeny. His *Boris Godou-noff* was the first of the nationalist operas, written outside Germany, which showed a way out of the Wagnerian impasse. *Boris* is operatic in the best sense of the word. Its main protagonist is the chorus rather than the individual; it derives its color from Russian locale; its musical background is freshened by the use of typically Russian folk-song material. The scene of the second tableau, which pictures the court of the Kremlin backed by the Czar's apartments, with the coronation procession crossing the stage, is one of the most spectacular ever conceived in the operatic medium.

The influence of *Boris* was only slowly felt, for it was not performed in Western Europe until the present century. But Debussy must have known of its existence during the visits that he made to Russia in early manhood. In any case, the influence of Moussorgsky is patent in Debussy's only opera, *Pelléas et Mélisande*, which is the next great landmark in operatic history. In *Pelléas*, Debussy returned to the Monteverdian ideal of opera; the words of Maeterlinck's poetic drama were given their full rights. The music was intended only to serve as a frame about the words, so as to heighten their poetic meaning.

In method and feeling, Debussy's opera was the antithesis of Wagnerian music drama. This is immediately seen if we compare the big scene in *Tristan* with the analogous one in *Pelléas*. In Wagner's opera, when the lovers declare themselves for the first time, there is a wonderful outpouring of the emotions in music; but when Pelléas and Mélisande first declare their love for each other, there is complete silence. Everyone—singers, orchestra, and composer—is overcome with emotion. That scene is typical of the whole opera—it is a triumph of understatement. There are very few forte passages in *Pelléas;* the entire work is bathed in an atmosphere of mystery and poignancy. Debussy's music added a new dimension to Maeterlinck's little play. It is impossible any longer to imagine the play apart from the music.

Perhaps it is just because of this complete identity of play and music that *Pelléas et Mélisande* has remained something of a special case. It provided no new program for the production of further operas in the same tradition. (Few other plays are so well designed for musical setting.) Moreover, the appeal of *Pelléas* was largely confined to those who understand French, since so much of the quality of the work is dependent on an understanding of the words. Because *Pelléas* had almost no offspring, the leaders of musical opinion lost interest in the operatic form altogether and turned instead to the symphony or the ballet as the principal musical form.

Reasons have already been given for the revival of interest in opera around 1924. All the operas written since then are in full reaction against Wagnerian ideals. Opera composers of today are agreed on at least one point: They are ready to accept frankly the conventions of the operatic stage. Since there is no possible hope of making opera "real," they have willingly renounced all attempt at reform. They bravely start from the premise that opera is a nonrealistic form, and, instead of deploring that fact, they are determined to make use of it. They are convinced that opera is, first of all, theater and that, as such, it demands a composer who is capable of writing stage music.

The most significant modern opera since *Pelléas* is, in the opinion of most critics, Alban Berg's *Wozzeck*. Berg's opera is striking on several counts. He, like Debussy, began with a stage play. *Wozzeck* was the work of a precocious nineteenth-century playwright, George Büchner. He tells the story, in 26 short scenes, of a poor devil of a soldier, at the bottom of the social scale, who through no fault of his own lives in misery and leaves nothing but a trail of misery behind him. This is a realistic theme, with social implications; but as Berg treated it, it became realism with a difference.

Opera and Music Drama

The impression that we get is one of a heightened, what is sometimes called an expressionistic, realism. Everything in the opera is extremely condensed. One swift scene follows another, each relating some essential dramatic moment, and all connected and focused through Berg's intensely expressive music.

One of the reasons for the slow acceptance in musical circles of this original work is the language of the music itself. Berg, as a devoted pupil of Arnold Schoenberg, made use of the atonal harmonic scheme of his teacher. *Wozzeck* was the first atonal opera to reach the stage. It is indicative of the dramatic power of the music that despite the fact of its being difficult to perform and almost as difficult to understand, it has made its way in both Europe and America. One other curious feature should be mentioned, which is found in *Wozzeck* and in the last work that Berg finished before his death, his second opera *Lulu*. Berg had the somewhat strange notion of introducing strict concert-hall forms, such as the passacaglia or rondo, into the body of his operas. This innovation in operatic form has no more than a technical interest, since the public hears the work with no idea of the presence of these underlying forms, this, according to the composer's own admission, being exactly his intention. Like every other opera, Berg's work holds the stage by virtue of its dramatic power.

A few modern operas have taken hold of the public imagination because of their treatment of some contemporary subject. The first of these was Krenek's *Jonny spielt auf*, which enjoyed an enormous vogue for a time. It seemed quite piquant to the provincial public of Germany that the hero of an opera should be a Negro jazz-band leader and that the composer should dare to introduce a few jazz tunes into his score.

Kurt Weill developed that popularizing tendency in a series that made opera history in pre-Hitler Germany. His most characteristic work of that period was the *Three Penny Opera*, with a telling libretto by Bert Brecht. Weill openly substituted "songs" for arias and a pseudo-jazz band for the usual opera orchestra and wrote a music so ordinary and trite that before long every German newsboy was whistling it. But what gives his work a distinction that *Jonny spielt auf* did not have was the fact that he wrote music of real character. It is a searing expression in musical terms of the German spirit of the 1920's, the hopelessly disintegrated and degenerated postwar Germany that George Grosz painted with brutal frankness. Do not be fooled by Weill's banality. It is a purposeful and meaningful banality if one can read between the lines, as it were, and sense the deep tragedy hidden in its seemingly carefree quality.

Opera as a comment on the social scene was once more demonstrated by the Italian-American composer Gian-Carlo Menotti in his *The Consul*. How long this tendency will continue is difficult to prophesy. But unless composers are able to universalize their comment and present it in terms of effective stage drama, no good will have come from bringing opera closer to everyday life.

This discussion of modern opera would be incomplete without some mention of one of the most prolific of contemporary opera composers, the Frenchman Darius Milhaud. Milhaud's most ambitious effort in this field has been his opera *Christopher Columbus*, a grandiose and spectacular affair which has had several productions abroad but none in this country. Milhaud can be violent and lyrical by turns, and he has used both qualities to good effect in *The Poor Sailor*, *Esther of Carpentras*, *Juarez and Maximilian*, and other stage works. A good idea of his dramatic power may be had from listening to an excerpt available on records, from his *Les Choephores*, called *Invocation*. Singer and chorus rhythmically declaim to the accompaniment of a whole battery of percussion instruments. The effect is quite overwhelming and points to new, unplumbed possibilities for the opera of the future.

If any of my readers still doubt the viability of modern opera or, for that matter, theatrical music in general, I ask them to consider this final fact. Three of the works that proved to be milestones in the development of new music were works designed for the stage. Moussorgsky's *Boris*, Debussy's *Pelléas*, and Stravinsky's *Rites of Spring* have all contributed to the advance of music. It may very well be that the next step forward will be made in the theater rather than the concert hall.

There still remains the question of opera in America or, to be more exact, American opera. Some of our writers have advanced the theory, with a good deal of reason, that the movies legitimately take the place of opera in the American scene. To them, opera is a typically European manifestation of art, not to be transplanted to American soil. But from the composer's standpoint, the opera is still a fascinating form, no matter how one looks at it. If it is to be transplanted with any chance of real success, two things must happen: Composers must be able to set English to a melodic line that does not falsify the natural rhythm of the language; and opera performances will have to be more numerous than they are at present in our country. As

a matter of fact, some of the healthiest of native operatic ventures, such as the Thomson-Stein *Four Saints
in Three Acts* or Marc Blitzstein's *The Cradle Will Rock*,
found their way on to the stage without benefit of an
established opera organization. Perhaps the future of
American opera lies *outside* the opera house. But in any
event, I feel sure we have not heard the last of the form,
either here or abroad.

16

Contemporary Music

O VER AND OVER again the question arises as to why it is that so many music lovers feel disoriented when they listen to contemporary music. They seem to accept with equanimity the notion that the work of the present-day composer is not for them. Why? Because they "just don't understand it." As a nonprofessional phrased it recently, "Far too many listeners still flinch when they are told that a piece of music is

Contemporary Music

'modern.'" Formerly—up to the middle twenties or thereabouts—all new music of progressive tendency was bunched together under the heading "ultramodern." Even today there still persists the idea that "classic" and "modern" represent two irreconcilable musical styles, the one posing graspable problems and the other fairly bristling with insoluble ones.

The first thing to remember is that creative artists, by and large, are a serious lot—their purpose is not to fool you. This, in turn, presupposes on your part an open mind, good will, and a certain a priori confidence in what they are up to. Composers vary greatly in range and scope, in temperament and in expression. Because of that, contemporary music imparts not one kind, but many different kinds of musical experience. That too is important to remember. Some present-day composers are very easy to understand, others may be very tough. Or different pieces by the same composer may fit into one or the other category. In between are a great many contemporary writers who range from being quite approachable to being fairly difficult.

To label all this music under the one heading "modern" is patently unfair, and can lead only to confusion. It might be helpful, therefore, to bring some order into the apparent chaos of contemporary composition by dividing some of its leading exponents according to the relative degree of difficulty in the understanding of their respective idioms:

Very easy: Shostakovitch and Khachaturian, Francis Poulenc and Erik Satie, early Stravinsky and Schoenberg, Virgil Thomson.

Quite approachable: Prokofieff, Villa-Lobos, Ernest Bloch, Roy Harris, William Walton, Malipiero, Britten.

Fairly difficult: Late Stravinsky, Béla Bartók, Milhaud, Chávez, William Schuman, Honegger, Hindemith, Walter Piston.

Very tough:: Middle and late Schoenberg, Alban Berg, Anton Webern, Varèse, Dallapiccola, Křenek, Roger Sessions, sometimes Charles Ives.

It is not at all essential that you agree with my comparative estimates. These are meant merely to indicate that not all new music ought to be thought of as equally inaccessible. The dodecaphonic school of Schoenberg is the hardest nut to crack, even for musicians. For the later Stravinsky you need a love of style, precision, personality; for Milhaud or Chávez a taste for sharply seasoned sonorities. Hindemith and Piston demand a contrapuntal ear; Poulenc and Thomson a witty intelligence; and Villa-Lobos a feeling for the lushly colorful.

[244]

Contemporary Music

The first essential, then, is to differentiate composers, trying to hear each separately in terms of what he wishes to communicate. Composers are not interchangeable! Each has his own objective and the wise listener would do well to keep that objective in the front of his mind.

This clarification of objective should also be borne in mind when we distinguish between the musical pleasures to be derived from old and new music. The uninitiated music lover will continue to find contemporary music peculiar so long as he persists in trying to hear the same kinds of sounds or derive the same species of musical enjoyment that he gets from the great works of past masters. This point is crucial. My love of the music of Chopin and Mozart is as strong as that of the next fellow, but it does me little good when I sit down to write my own, because their world is not mine and their musical language not mine. The underlying principles of their music are just as cogent today as they were in their own period, but with these same principles one may and one does produce a quite different result. When approaching a present-day musical work of serious pretensions, one must first realize what the objective of the composer is and then expect to hear a different sort of treatment than was customary in the past.

What to Listen for in Music

In dealing with the elements and forms of music, various instances were cited to show how recent composers have adapted and extended our technical resources for their own expressive purposes. These extensions of conventional procedures necessarily imply the ability, on the listener's part, to lend himself by instinct or training to the unfamiliar idiom. If, for example, you find yourself rejecting music because it is too dissonant, it probably indicates that your ear is insufficiently accustomed to our present-day musical vocabulary, and needs more practice—that is, training in listening. (There is always the possibility that the composer himself may be at fault through the writing of uninspired or willful dissonances.)

In following a new work, the melodic content—or seeming lack of it—may be a source of confusion. You may very well miss hearing the straightforward tune that can be hummed. Melodies nowadays can be "unsingable," especially in instrumental writing, if only because they go far beyond the limitations of the human voice. Or it may be that they are too tortuous, or jagged, or fragmentary to have any immediacy of appeal. These are expressive attributes that may, temporarily, perplex the listener. But the composer, given the expanded scope of contemporary melodic invention, cannot return to the plain and sometimes obvious melody writing of an earlier day. Assuming a gifted composer, repeated hearings should make clear the long-range appeal of his more intricate line.

Finally there is the reproach that is repeated more often than any other, namely, that today's music appears to avoid sentiment and feeling, that it is merely cerebral and clever rather than emotionally meaningful. A brief paragraph can hardly hope to deal adequately with this persistent misconception. If a contemporary composer's work strikes you as cold and intellectual, ask yourself if you are not using standards of comparison that really do not apply. Most music lovers do not appreciate to what an extent they are under the spell of the romantic approach to music. Our audiences have come to identify nineteenth-century musical romanticism as analogous to the art of music itself. Because romanticism was, and still remains, so powerful an expression, they tend to forget that great music was written for hundreds of years before the romantics flourished.

It so happens that a considerable proportion of today's music has closer aesthetic ties with that earlier music than it has with the romantics. The way of the uninhibited and personalized warmth and surge of the best of the romanticists is not our way. Even that segment of contemporary composition that clearly has romantic overtones is careful to express itself more discreetly, without exaggeration. And so it must, for the self-evident truth is that the romantic movement had reached its apogee by the end of the last century and nothing fresh was to be extracted from it.

The transition from romanticism to a more objective musical ideal was a gradual one. Since composers themselves found it difficult to make the break, it is not to be wondered at that the public at large has been slow to accept the full implication of what has been happening. The nineteenth century was the romantic century par excellence—a romanticism that found its most characteristic expression in the art of music. Perhaps that explains the continued reluctance of the music-loving public to admit that with the new century a different kind of music had to come into being. And yet their counterparts in the literary world do not expect André Gide or Thomas Mann or T. S. Eliot to emote with the accents of Victor Hugo or Sir Walter Scott. Why then should Bartók or Sessions be expected to sing with the voice of Brahms or Tschaikovsky? When a contemporary piece seems dry and cerebral to you, when it seems to be giving off little feeling or sentiment, there is a good chance that you are being insensitive to the characteristic musical speech of your own epoch.

Contemporary Music

That musical speech—if it is truly vital—is certain to include an experimental and controversial side. And why not? Why is it that the typical music lover of our day is seemingly so reluctant to consider a musical composition as, possibly, a challenging experience? When I hear a new piece of music that I do not understand, I am intrigued—I want to make contact with it again at the first opportunity. It's a challenge—it keeps my interest in the art of music thoroughly alive. If, after repeated hearings, a work says nothing to me, I do not therefore conclude that modern composition is in a sorry condition. I simply conclude that that piece is not for me.

I've sadly observed, however, that my own reaction is not typical. Most people seem to resent the controversial in music; they don't want their listening habits disturbed. They use music as a couch; they want to be pillowed on it, relaxed and consoled for the stress of daily living. But serious music was never meant to be used as a soporific. Contemporary music, especially, is created to wake you up, not put you to sleep. It is meant to stir and excite you, to move you—it may even exhaust you. But isn't that the kind of stimulation you go to the theater for or read a book for? Why make an exception for music?

It may be that new music sounds peculiar for the

sole reason that, in the course of ordinary listening, one hears so little of it by comparison with the amount of conventional music that is performed year in and year out. Radio and concert programs, the advertisements of the record manufacturers and their dealers, the usual school curricula—all emphasize the idea, unwittingly, perhaps, that "normal" music is music of the past, music that has proved its worth. A generous estimate indicates that only one-quarter of the music we hear can be called contemporary—and that estimate applies mostly to music heard in the larger musical centers. Under such circumstances contemporary music is likely to remain "peculiar," unless the listener is willing to make the extra effort needed to break the barrier of unfamiliarity.

To feel no need of involvement in the musical expression of one's own day is to shut oneself off from one of the most exciting experiences the art of music can provide. Contemporary music speaks to us as no other music can. It is the older music—the music of Buxtehude and Cherubini—that should seem distant and foreign to us, not that of Milhaud and William Schuman. But isn't music universal? What, you may ask, does the living composer say that will not be found in somewhat analogous terms in an earlier music? All depends on the angle of vision: what we see produces

[250]

Contemporary Music

wider extremes of tension and release, a more vivid optimism, a grayer pessimism, climaxes of abandonment and explosive hysteria, coloristic variety—subtleties of light and dark, a relaxed sense of fun sometimes spilling over into the grotesque, crowded textures, open-spaced vistas, "painful" longing, dazzling brilliance. Various shades and gradations of these moods have their counterpart in older music, no doubt, but no sensitive listener would ever confuse the two. We usually recognize the period a composition belongs in as an essential part of its physiognomy. It is the uniqueness of any authentic art expression that makes even approximate duplication in any other period inconceivable. That is why the music lover who neglects contemporary music deprives himself of the enjoyment of an otherwise unobtainable aesthetic experience.

The key to the understanding of new music is repeated hearings. Fortunately for us, the prevalence of the long-play disk makes this entirely possible. Many listeners have attested to the fact that incomprehensibility gradually gives way before the familiarity that only repeated hearing can give. There is, in any event, no better way to test whether contemporary music is to have significance for you.

17

Film Music

FILM MUSIC constitutes a new musical medium that exerts a fascination of its own. Actually, it is a new form of dramatic music—related to opera, ballet, incidental theater music—in contradistinction to concert music of the symphonic or chamber-music kind. As a new form it opens up unexplored possibilities for composers and poses some interesting questions for the musical film patron.

[252]

Film Music

Millions of movie-goers take the musical accompaniment to a dramatic film entirely too much for granted. Five minutes after the termination of a picture they couldn't tell you whether they heard music or not. To ask whether they thought the score exciting or merely adequate or downright awful would be to give them a musical inferiority complex. But, on second thought, and possibly in self-protection, comes the query: "Isn't it true that one isn't supposed to be listening to the music? Isn't it supposed to work on you unconsciously without being listened to directly as you would listen at a concert?"

No discussion of movie music ever gets very far without having to face this problem: Should one hear a movie score? If you are a musician there is no problem because the chances are you can't help but listen. More than once a good picture has been ruined for me by an inferior score. Have you had the same experience? Yes? Then you may congratulate yourself: you are definitely musical.

But it's the average spectator, so absorbed in the dramatic action that he fails to take in the background music, who wants to know whether he is missing anything. The answer is bound up with the degree of your general musical perception. It is the degree to which you are aurally minded that will determine how much pleasure you may derive by absorbing the background musical accompaniment as an integral part of the combined impression made by the film.

Knowing more of what goes into the scoring of a picture may help the movie listener to get more out of it. Fortunately, the process is not so complex that it cannot be briefly outlined.

In preparation for composing the music, the first thing the composer must do, of course, is to see the picture. Almost all musical scores are written *after* the film itself is completed. The only exception to this is when the script calls for realistic music—that is, music which is visually sung or played or danced to on the screen. In that case the music must be composed before the scene is photographed. It will then be recorded and the scene in question shot to a playback of the recording. Thus when you see an actor singing or playing or dancing, he is only making believe as far as the sound goes, for the music had previously been put down in recorded form.

The first run-through of the film for the composer is usually a solemn moment. After all, he must live with it for several weeks. The solemnity of the occasion is emphasized by the exclusive audience that views it with him: the producer, the director, the music head of the studio, the picture editor, the music cutter, the

Film Music

conductor, the orchestrater—in fact, anyone involved with the scoring of the picture.

The purpose of the run-through is to decide how much music is needed and where it should be. (In technical jargon this is called "to spot" the picture.) Since no background score is continuous throughout the full length of a film (that would constitute a motion-picture opera, an almost unexploited cinema form), the score will normally consist of separate sequences, each lasting from a few seconds to several minutes in duration. A sequence as long as seven minutes would be exceptional. The entire score, made up of perhaps thirty or more such sequences, may add up to from forty to ninety minutes of music.

Much discussion, much give-and-take may be necessary before final decisions are reached regarding the "spotting" of the picture. It is wise to make use of music's power sparingly, saving it for absolutely essential points. A composer knows how to play with silences—knows that to take music out can at times be more effective than any use of it on the sound track might be.

The producer-director, on the other hand, is more prone to think of music in terms of its immediate functional usage. Sometimes he has ulterior motives: anything wrong with a scene—a poor bit of acting, a badly read line, an embarrassing pause—he secretly hopes will be covered up by a clever composer. Producers have been known to hope that an entire picture would be saved by a good score. But the composer is not a magician; he can hardly be expected to do more than to make potent through music the film's dramatic and emotional values.

When well-contrived, there is no question but that a musical score can be of enormous help to a picture. One can prove that point, laboratory-fashion, by showing an audience a climactic scene with the sound turned off and then once again with the sound track turned on. Here briefly are listed a number of ways in which music serves the screen:

1. *Creating a more convincing atmosphere of time and place.* Not all Hollywood composers bother about this nicety. Too often, their scores are interchangeable: a thirteenth-century Gothic drama and a hard-boiled modern battle of the sexes get similar treatment. The lush symphonic texture of late nineteenth-century music remains the dominating influence. But there are exceptions. Recently, the higher-grade horse opera has begun to have its own musical flavor, mostly a folksong derivative.

2. *Underlining psychological refinements—the unspoken thoughts of a character or the unseen implications of a situ-*

ation. Music can play upon the emotions of the spectator, sometimes counterpointing the thing seen with an aural image that implies the contrary of the thing seen. This is not as subtle as it sounds. A well-placed dissonant chord can stop an audience cold in the middle of a sentimental scene, or a calculated woodwind passage can turn what appears to be a solemn moment into a belly laugh.

3. *Serving as a kind of neutral background filler.* This is really the music one isn't supposed to hear, the sort that helps to fill the empty spots, such as pauses in a conversation. It's the movie composer's most ungrateful task. But at times, though no one else may notice, he will get private satisfaction from the thought that music of little intrinsic value, through professional manipulation, has enlivened and made more human the deathly pallor of a screen shadow. This is hardest to do, as any film composer will attest, when the neutral filler type of music must weave its way underneath dialogue.

4. *Building a sense of continuity.* The picture editor knows better than anyone how serviceable music can be in tying together a visual medium which is, by its very nature, continually in danger of falling apart. One sees this most obviously in montage scenes where the use of a unifying musical idea may save the quick

flashes of disconnected scenes from seeming merely chaotic.

5. *Underpinning the theatrical build-up of a scene, and rounding it off with a sense of finality.* The first instance that comes to mind is the music that blares out at the end of a film. Certain producers have boasted their picture's lack of a musical score, but I never saw or heard of a picture that ended in silence.

We have merely skimmed the surface, without mentioning the innumerable examples of utilitarian music—offstage street bands, the barn dance, merry-go-rounds, circus music, café music, the neighbor's girl practicing her piano, and the like. All these, and many others, introduced with apparent naturalistic intent, serve to vary subtly the aural interest of the sound track.

But now let us return to our hypothetical composer. Having determined where the separate musical sequences will begin and end, he turns the film over to the music cutter, who prepares a so-called cue sheet. The cue sheet provides the composer with a detailed description of the physical action in each sequence, plus the exact timings in thirds of seconds of that action, thereby making it possible for a practiced composer to write an entire score without ever again referring to the picture.

Film Music

The layman usually imagines that the most difficult part of the job in composing for the films has to do with the precise "fitting" of the music to the action. Doesn't that kind of timing strait-jacket the composer? The answer is no, for two reasons: First, having to compose music to accompany specific action is a help rather than a hindrance, since the action itself induces music in a composer of theatrical imagination, whereas he has no such visual stimulus in writing absolute music. Secondly, the timing is mostly a matter of minor adjustments, since the over-all musical fabric will have already been determined.

For the composer of concert music, changing to the medium of celluloid does bring certain special pitfalls. For example, melodic invention, highly prized in the concert hall, may at times be distracting in certain film situations. Even phrasing in the concert manner, which would normally emphasize the independence of separate contrapuntal lines, may be distracting when applied to screen accompaniments. In orchestration there are many subtleties of timbre—distinctions meant to be listened to for their own expressive quality in an auditorium—which are completely wasted on sound track.

As compensation for these losses, the composer has other possibilities, some of them tricks, which are unobtainable in Carnegie Hall. In scoring one section of *The Heiress*, for example, I was able to superimpose two orchestras, one upon another. Both recorded the same music at different times, one orchestra consisting of strings alone, the other constituted normally. Later these were combined by simultaneously rerecording the original tracks, thereby producing a highly expressive orchestral texture. Bernard Herrmann, one of the most ingenious of screen composers, called for (and got) eight celestas—an unheard-of combination on 57th Street—to suggest a winter's sleigh ride. Miklos Rozsa's use of the "echo chamber"—a device to give normal tone a ghostlike aura—was widely remarked, and subsequently done to death.

Unusual effects are obtainable through overlapping incoming and outgoing music tracks. Like two trains passing one another, it is possible to bring in and take out at the same time two different musics. *The Red Pony* gave me an opportunity to use this cinema specialty. When the daydreaming imagination of a little boy turns white chickens into white circus horses the visual image is mirrored in an aural image by having the chicken music transform itself into circus music, a device only obtainable by means of the overlap.

Let us now assume that the musical score has been completed and is ready for recording. The scoring stage

Film Music

is a happy-making place for the composer. Hollywood has gathered to itself some of America's finest performers; the music will be beautifully played and recorded with a technical perfection not to be matched anywhere else.

Most composers like to invite their friends to be present at the recording session of important sequences. The reason is that neither the composer nor his friends are ever again likely to hear the music sound out in concert style. For when it is combined with the picture most of the dynamic levels will be changed. Otherwise the finished product might sound like a concert with pictures. In lowering dynamic levels niceties of shading, some inner voices and bass parts may be lost. Erich Korngold put it well when he said: "A movie composer's immortality lasts from the recording stage to the dubbing room."

The dubbing room is where all the tracks involving sound of any kind, including dialogue, are put through the machines to obtain one master sound track. This is a delicate process as far as the music is concerned, for it is only a hairbreadth that separates the "too loud" from the "too soft." Sound engineers, working the dials that control volume, are not always as musically sensitive as composers would like them to be. What is called for is a new species, a sound mixer who is half musician and half engineer; and even then, the mixing of dialogue, music, and realistic sounds of all kinds must always remain problematical.

In view of these drawbacks to the full sounding out of his music, it is only natural that the composer often hopes to be able to extract a viable concert suite from his film score. There is a current tendency to believe that movie scores are not proper material for concert music. The argument is that, separated from its visual justification, the music falls flat.

Personally, I doubt very much that any hard and fast rule can be made that will cover all cases. Each score will have to be judged on its merits, and, no doubt, stories that require a more continuous type of musical development in a unified atmosphere will lend themselves better than others to reworking for concert purposes. Rarely is it conceivable that the music of a film might be extracted without much reworking. But I fail to see why, if successful suites like Grieg's *Peer Gynt* can be made from nineteenth-century incidental stage music, a twentieth-century composer can't be expected to do as well with a film score.

As for the picture score, it is only in the motion-picture theater that the composer for the first time gets the full impact of what he has accomplished, tests the dramatic punch of his favorite spot, appreciates the cu-

Film Music

rious importance and unimportance of detail, wishes that he had done certain things differently, and is surprised that others came off better than he had hoped. For when all is said and done, the art of combining moving pictures with musical tones is still a mysterious art. Not the least mysterious element is the theatergoers' reaction: Millions will be listening but one never knows how many will be really hearing. The next time you go to the movies, remember to be on the composer's side.

18

From Composer to Interpreter
to Listener

T HUS far, this book has been largely concerned with music in the abstract. But, practically considered, almost every musical situation implies three distinct factors: a composer, an interpreter, and a listener. They form a triumvirate, no part of which is complete without the other. Music begins with a composer; passes through the medium of an interpreter; and ends with you, the listener. Everything in music

[264]

From Composer to Interpreter to Listener

may be said, in the final analysis, to be directed at you—the listener. Therefore, to listen intelligently, you must clearly understand not only your own role but also that of composer and interpreter and what each one contributes to the sum total of a musical experience.

Let us begin with the composer, since music in our own civilization begins with him. What, after all, do we listen for when we listen to a composer? He need not tell us a story like the novelist; he need not "copy" nature like the sculptor; his work need have no immediate practical function like the architect's drawing. What is it that he gives us, then? Only one answer seems possible to me: He gives us himself. Every artist's work is, of course, an expression of himself, but none so direct as that of the creative musician. He gives us, without relation to exterior "events," the quintessential part of himself—that part which embodies the fullest and deepest expression of himself as a man and of his experience as a fellow being.

Always remember that when you listen to a composer's creation you are listening to a man, to a particular individual, with his own special personality. For a composer, to be of any value, must have his own personality. It may be of greater or lesser importance, but, in the case of significant music, it will always mirror that personality. No composer can write into his music a value that he does not possess as a man. His character may be streaked with human frailties—like Lully's or Wagner's, for example—but whatever is fine in his music will come from whatever is fine in him as a man.

If we examine this question of the composer's individual character more closely, we shall discover that it is really made up of two distinct elements: the personality with which he was born and the influences of the time in which he lives. For, obviously, every composer lives in a certain period, and each period has its character, too. Whatever personality a composer may have is expressed within the framework of his own period. It is the interreaction of personality and period that results in the formation of a composer's style. Two composers with exactly similar personalities living in two different epochs would inevitably produce music of two different styles. When we speak of a composer's style, therefore, we refer to the combined result of an individual character and a particular period.

Perhaps this important question of musical style will be made clearer if applied to a specific case. Take Beethoven, for example. One of the most obvious characteristics of his style is its ruggedness. Beethoven, as a man, had the reputation of being a brusque and rugged individual. From the testimony of the music alone, however, we know him to be a composer with a bold, uncouth quality, the very antithesis of the suave and the mellifluous. Still, that rugged character of Beethoven's took on a different expression at different periods of his life. The ruggedness of the *First Symphony* is different from that of the *Ninth*. It is a difference of periods. The early Beethoven was rugged within the limits of an eighteenth-century classical manner, whereas the mature Beethoven underwent the influence of the liberating tendencies of the nineteenth century. That is why, in considering the style of a composer, we must take into account his personality as reflected by the period in which he lived. There are as many styles as there are composers, and each important composer has several different styles corresponding to the influences of his own time and the maturing of his own personality.

If it is essential for the listener to understand the question of musical style as applied to a composer's work, it is even more so for the interpreter. For the interpreter is a kind of middleman in music. It is not so much the composer that the listener hears, as the interpreter's conception of the composer. The writer's contact with his reader is direct; the painter's picture need only be hung well to be seen. But music, like the

[267]

theater, is an art that must be reinterpreted in order to live. The poor composer, having finished his composition, must turn it over to the tender mercies of an interpretive artist—who, it must always be remembered, is a being with his own musical nature and his own personality. The lay listener, therefore, can judge an interpretation fairly only if he is able to distinguish between the composer's thought, ideally speaking, and the degree to which the interpreter is faithfully reproducing that thought.

The role of the interpreter leaves no room for argument. All are agreed that he exists to serve the composer—to assimilate and recreate the composer's "message." The theory is plain enough—it is its practical application that needs elucidation.

Most first-rate interpretive artists today possess a technical equipment that is more than sufficient for any demands made upon them. So that in most cases we can take technical proficiency for granted. The first real interpretive problem is presented by the notes themselves. Musical notation, as it exists today, is not an exact transcription of a composer's thought. It cannot be, for it is too vague; it allows for too great a leeway in individual matters of taste and choice. Because of that, the interpreter is forever confronted with the problem of how literally he is expected to keep to the printed page. Composers are only human—they have been known to put notes down inexactly, to overlook important omissions. They have also been known to change their opinions in regard to their own indications of tempo or dynamics. Interpreters, therefore, must use their musical intelligence before the printed page. There is, of course, the possibility of exaggeration in both directions—keeping too strictly to the notes or straying too far away from them. The problem would probably be solved, up to a certain point, if a more exact way of noting down a composition were available. But, even so, music would still be open to a number of different interpretations.

For a composition is, after all, an organism. It is a living, not a static, thing. That is why it is capable of being seen in a different light and from different angles by various interpreters or even by the same interpreter at different times. Interpretation is, to a large extent, a matter of emphasis. Every piece has an essential quality which the interpretation must not betray. It takes its quality from the nature of the music itself, which is derived from the personality of the composer himself and the period in which it was written. In other words, every composition has its own style which the interpreter must be faithful to. But every interpreter has his own personality, too, so that we hear

the style of a piece as refracted by the personality of
the interpreter.

The relation of the performer to the composition that
he is recreating is therefore a delicate one. When the
interpreter injects his personality into a performance
to an unwarranted degree, misunderstandings arise. In
recent years, the mere word "interpretation" has fallen
into disrepute. Discouraged and disgruntled by the ex-
aggerations and falsifications of "prima donna" interpreters, a certain number of composers, with
Stravinsky as ringleader, have, in effect, said: "We do
not wish any so-called interpretations of our music; just
play the notes; add nothing, and take nothing away."
Though the reason for this admonishment is clear
enough, it seems to me to represent a nonrealistic attitude on the part of composers. For no finished interpreter can possibly play a piece of music or even a
phrase, for that matter, without adding something of
his or her own personality. To have it otherwise, interpreters would have to be automatons. Inevitably,
when they perform music, they perform it in their own
way. In doing so, they need not falsify the composer's
intentions; they are merely "reading" it with the in-
flections of their own voice.

But there are further, and more profound, reasons
for differences in interpretation. There is no doubt that

[270]

From Composer to Interpreter to Listener

a Brahms symphony, interpreted by two first-rate conductors, may be different in effect without being unfaithful to Brahms' intentions. It is interesting to ruminate on why that should be true.

Take, for example, two of the outstanding interpreters of our day—Arturo Toscanini and Serge Koussevitzky.* They are two entirely different personalities—men who think differently, who emotionalize about things in a different way, whose philosophy of life is different. It is only to be expected that in handling the same notes their interpretations will vary considerably.

The Italian conductor is a classicist by nature. A certain detachment is an essential part of the classicist's make-up. One's first impression is a curious one—Toscanini seems to be doing nothing at all to the music. It is only after one has listened for a while that the sense of an art concealing art begins to take hold of one. He treats the music as if it were an object. It seems to exist at the back of the stage—where we can contemplate it for our pleasure. There is a wonderful sense of detachment about it. Yet all the time it is music, the most passionate of all the arts. The emphasis with Toscanini is always on the line, on the structure as a whole—never on detail or on the separate measure. The

*This comparison of personality traits was written during their years as active interpreters of symphonic literature.

music moves and lives for its own sake, and we are considered fortunate in being able to contemplate it living thus.

The Russian conductor, on the other hand, is a romanticist by nature. He is involved, body and soul, in the music that he interprets. There is little of the calculative about him. He possesses the true romanticist's fire, passion, dramatic imagination, and sensuosity. With Koussevitzky every masterpiece is a battleground on which he captains the great fight, and out of which, you may be sure, the human spirit will emerge triumphant. When he is "in the mood," the effect is overwhelming.

When these two opposite personalities apply their gifts to the same Brahms symphony, the result is bound to be different. This case of a profoundly German composer's being interpreted by a Russian and an Italian is typical. Neither one is likely to produce a quality of sound from his orchestra that a German would recognize as *echt deutsch*. In the Russian's hands, Brahms's orchestra will glow with an unsuspected luster, and every ounce of romantic drama that the symphony contains will be extracted by the time the end has been reached. With the Italian, on the other hand, the structural-classical side of Brahms will be stressed, and the melodic lines will be etched in the purest of lyrical styles. In both cases, as you see, it is simply a question of emphasis. It may be that neither of these men is your idea of the perfect interpreter of a Brahms symphony. But that is not the point. The point is that in order to hear an interpretation intelligently, you must be able to recognize what, exactly, the interpreter is doing to the composition at the moment that he recreates it.

In other words, you must become more aware of the interpreter's part in the performance you are hearing. To do that, two things are necessary: You must have, as point of reference, a more or less ideal conception of the style that is proper to the composer in question; and you must be able to sense to what degree the interpreter is reproducing that style, within the sphere of his own personality. However short any of us may fall from attaining this ideal in listening, it is well that we keep it in mind as an objective.

By now, the importance of the listener's role in this whole process must be self-evident. The combined efforts of composer and interpreter have meaning only in so far as they go out to an intelligent body of hearers. That bespeaks a responsibility on the part of the hearer. But before one can understand music, one must really love it. Above all things, composers and interpreters want listeners who lend themselves fully to the music that they are hearing. Virgil Thomson once described the ideal listener as "a person who applauds vigorously." By that *bon mot* he meant to imply, no doubt, that only a listener who really involves himself is of importance to music or the makers of music.

To lend oneself completely inevitably means, for one thing, the broadening of one's taste. It is insufficient to love music only in its more conventional aspects. Taste, like sensitivity, is, to a certain extent, an inborn quality, but both can be considerably developed by intelligent practice. That means listening to music of all schools and all periods, old and new, conservative and modern. It means unprejudiced listening in the best sense of the term.

Take seriously your responsibility as listener. All of us, professionals and laymen alike, are forever striving to make our understanding of the art more profound. You need be no exception, no matter how modest your pretensions as listener may be. Since it is our combined reaction as listeners that most profoundly influences both the art of composition and interpretation, it may truthfully be said that the future of music is in our hands.

From Composer to Interpreter to Listener

Music can only be really alive when there are listeners who are really alive. To listen intently, to listen consciously, to listen with one's whole intelligence is the least we can do in the furtherance of an art that is one of the glories of mankind.

APPENDIX I

Typical Variation Formulas

THEME

Ach! du lieber Augustin

1. Harmonic variants:

    a. The melody is retained literally, but the accompanying harmonies are completely transformed:

Appendix

b. The melody and original chordal accompaniment are retained, but the texture becomes enriched:

Appendix

c. All trace of the melody is lost. Only the underlying harmonic skeleton is kept (in the case of
Ach! du lieber Augustin, only two chords are involved—tonic and dominant):

d. The chordal skeleton itself is varied. Here it is
not so much a variation of the theme as a variation of the accompanying chords of a theme:

2. Melodic variants:

a. The melody itself is varied. The outer contours
are kept, but the line is more florid. This type is
based on the fundamental concept in music that

Appendix

if you pass from C to D, you can also go by way
of C sharp (C-C#-D) without changing anything
essential to the line:

b. The second melodic type is the opposite of the
foregoing—making the melodic line less florid
than it is, by concentrating on the barest essential notes. In other words, if the original theme
passes from C to C sharp to D, the line may go
directly from C to D:

Appendix

c. The theme is retained, but its position is changed from upper to lower or middle part, or vice versa:

3. Rhythmic variant:

 a. All types of rhythmic variation may be grouped under one heading—rhythmic change. One example: if the three-quarter, waltz character of *Ach! du lieber Augustin* is changed to four-quarter in very fast tempo, the nature of the theme is completely transformed:

4. Contrapuntal variants:

   a. A simple type of contrapuntal variation consists
   of adding a new theme to the original, giving emphasis to the new one while retaining the original in the background:

b. A second, more subtle, scheme consists of extracting a single phrase from the original theme and subjecting it to contrapuntal treatment. This type is difficult for the listener to follow unless the derivation of the fragment is clear from the start:

5. Any combination of the foregoing types.

APPENDIX II

Contrapuntal Devices

1. Imitation (*Bach*—E♭ Minor Fugue, Well-Tempered Clavichord, Book I)

2. Canon (*outline*) (*Bach*—Erchienen ist der herrliche Tag)

Appendix

3. Inversion (*Beethoven*—Piano Sonata, Op. 110)

4. Augmentation (*Bach*—C minor fugue, Well-Tempered Clavichord, Book II)

5. Diminution (Scherzo—Symphony in F minor—*Vaughan-Williams*)

Permission for illustration 5 granted by Oxford University Press, London.

[284]

Appendix

6. Cancrizans (Passacaglia for Piano—*Copland*)

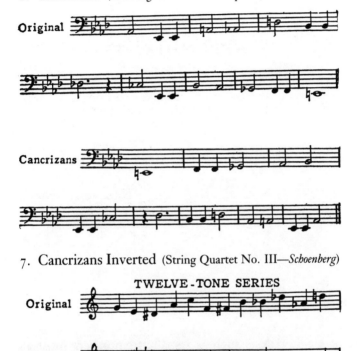

7. Cancrizans Inverted (String Quartet No. III—*Schoenberg*)

Permission for illustration 6 granted by Maurice Senart, Paris, and Elkan-Vogel Company, Inc., Philadelphia, copyright owners. Copyright assigned to Salabert & Co., New York.

APPENDIX III

Analysis of

BEETHOVEN'S "WALDSTEIN" SONATA, OP. 53

A<small>N ANALYSIS</small> such as I shall attempt here must always be unsatisfactory, since we lack the sound of the notes themselves. I shall proceed on the assumption, possibly unwarranted, that the reader can secure either the printed score or the recording.

One of the advantages of using this particular sonata as illustration of the form is the utter contrast between the first and second thematic groups. If you think only

Appendix

in terms of melody, the first theme is hardly a theme at all. It is made up of three separate tiny parts, producing an atmosphere of suspense and mysteriousness. It is the underlying rhythm in repeated eighth notes which is responsible for this and may be accounted the first element. The second element is harmless enough:

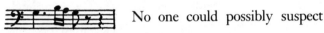 No one could possibly suspect

the role it is to play later in the development section. The same is true of the third tiny fragment, which is

as follows:

The first four measures are immediately repeated a tone below and without stopping rush forward to a complete pause on the note G (measure 13). Now, once again, everything is repeated from the start, with the important difference that the repeated eighth notes of the beginning are broken up into sixteenths (figurated) and slightly changed in tonality. These repetitions serve the important purpose of placing essential thematic material firmly in the listener's consciousness. This time there is no pause; the music, through a series of elongations, imperceptibly moves into the bridge section (measure 23, see page 186 for explanation of this term). What one finds here is not melody but

Appendix

runs and arpeggios—so-called passage work. Even if you never heard this sonata before, it would be clear from the nature of the material that the piece was moving on from a first to a second grouping of elements.

The transition in this case is really brilliantly accomplished! The music seems to slow itself up, in order to begin a second theme (measure 35) of a completely opposed nature. The slowly moving, sustained chords produce a chorale-like, almost religious feeling of calm and ease. These sustained chords are repeated immediately (measure 43), with the addition of a single florid melodic line above. (It is characteristic that despite the amount of repetition, so usual in all music, there is seldom *literal* repetition but repeated sections varied.)

That extra florid melody, woven above the sustained chords, acts as an "excuse" for returning to the more figurated character of the first transition section (measure 50). Here we have one of those tantalizing moments when the analyst is torn between different interpretations of the form. Obviously, this new passage work is one of two things: either it is a second part of *b*, which one is reluctant to admit, because it is so very different in nature from the first part of *b*; or it is a second bridge leading to *c*, which is rather unlikely because of its overelaborate nature. That is where

Appendix

the composer is fortunate—he never need give conscious reasons to himself for the form that he creates, if the end result is a logical one. But the poor theorist, if *he* wishes to explain the form, cannot very well do so without making up his mind. Therefore, I elect the first of these alternatives, preferring to consider this long passage-work section as a kind of *b*-2 which leads to the closing theme.

The *c*, or closing, section (measure 74), shorter than the others, has more affinity with the songlike second theme than with the agitated first theme. It serves to bring the mood back to a feeling of quietude, thereby emphasizing the sense of conclusion and at the same time preparing the way for the renewed entrance of the first material at the head of the development section.

That is exactly what happens. The first thing that the composer does is to remind you of where he began—to give you a point of reference, as it were. This is hardly done, before Beethoven is off! As a matter of fact, this particular development section is neither very long nor very elaborate. For development, it chooses only the two fragments quoted on the previous page and the section I elected to call *b*-2. No reference is made to the chorale-like theme or the closing theme or the opening repeated eighth notes. But there is a gen-

[289]

Appendix

eral feeling of movement and inner excitement, which pervades most of the whole first movement.

The development section is divided into two parts. First the composer juxtaposes the two fragments of the first theme quoted above (measure 92). Then he concentrates on the first of the two fragments, developing what was originally only a tiny phrase into a swiftly lyrical little part. This leads directly to the development of the next material—the opening measures of the *b*-2 passage work. On that basis, the music works itself out sequentially in such a way that a great many foreign tonalities are passed through before the dominant note G is reached. On this dominant (measure 142), Beethoven returns to the mysterious feeling of the very beginning in order to prepare psychologically for the return of the first theme. This retransition is quite remarkable, if only because it would be impossible to find anything comparable to it in the music of Haydn or Mozart. The *misterioso* rumblings in the bass and the gradual piling up of climax is typically Beethoven's touch.

With a sudden return to pianissimo, the recapitulation starts (measure 156). The repetition in this case is almost literal, except for a few very minor changes, mostly of tonalities. A two-and-a-half-page coda follows (measure 249). After beginning almost like the

Appendix

first development section, it goes on to a further development of the same two fragments used there but now juxtaposed in a somewhat different fashion. This leads back, after two held chords, to the chorale-like theme, made newly expressive by the addition of a new bass (measure 284). The seeming reluctance to leave this new-found quietude is broken off by an impetuous rush to the end. The sonata-allegro is completed.

List of Recorded Works

This list consists largely of those works cited as illustrations in the text that are now available on long-play records (1957). A few supplementary recordings have been mentioned, marked by an asterisk. No attempt has been made to recommend specific performances in preference to others. Competent books for that purpose are available.

List of Recorded Works

Chávez—*Sinfonia India*
Strauss—*Till Eulenspiegel's Merry Pranks*, Op. 28
Wagner—*Tristan und Isolde* (Prelude and *Liebestod*)
Harris—Trio for violin, cello, and piano
Prokofieff—Violin Concerto No. 2 in G minor (second movement)
*Berg—Concerto for Violin
*Schoenberg—*The Book of the Hanging Gardens*
CHAPTER 6. HARMONY
Masterpieces of Music before 1750 (organum)
Monteverdi—Madrigals
Gesualdo—Madrigals
Moussorgsky—*Songs and Dances of Death*
Debussy—*Iberia*
Schoenberg—*Five Orchestral Pieces*
Webern—*Five Movements for String Quartet*
Milhaud—*Saudades do Brazil* (especially "Corcovado")
*Dallapiccola—*Canti di Prigiona*
*Martin—*Petite Symphonie Concertante*
CHAPTER 7. TONE COLOR
Debussy—*Afternoon of a Faun*
Honegger—Concertino for Piano
Britten—*The Young Person's Guide to the Orchestra*, Op. 34
Ibert—Flute Concerto
Cimarosa—Oboe Concerto
Nielsen—Clarinet Concerto
Vivaldi—Bassoon Concerto
Mozart—Horn Concerto
Haydn—Trumpet Concerto
Hindemith—Trombone Sonata
Wagner—*Tristan und Isolde*, Prelude to Act III (English horn solo)
Ravel—*Mother Goose Suite* (contrabassoon in "Beauty and the Beast")
Moussorgsky-Ravel—*Pictures at an Exhibition* (tuba solo)
Ravel—*Bolero* (various instrumental solos)
Percussion Music: Bell, Drum, and Cymbal (Saul Goodman)

[293]

List of Recorded Works

First Chair (Philadelphia Orchestra, woodwind and brass solos)
Stan Kenton—*A Concert of Progressive Jazz*
Duke Ellington—*Duke Ellington Plays Duke Ellington*
CHAPTER 8. MUSICAL TEXTURE
Monophonic texture:
Gregorian Chant
Homophonic texture:
Monteverdi—*Il Combattimento di Tancredi e Clorinda*
Polyphonic texture:
*Bach—Musical Offering
Hindemith—*Das Marienleben*
Varied texture:
Beethoven—Symphony No. 7 (Allegretto movement)
CHAPTER 9. MUSICAL STRUCTURE
Schumann—*Scenes from Childhood (Kinderscenen)*, Op. 15
Beethoven—Piano Sonata, Op. 27, No. 2 (Scherzo)
CHAPTER 10. SECTIONAL FORM
Two-part form:
F. Couperin—Music for the Harpsichord (*Les Barricades mys-
térieuses, Le Moucheron, La Commère, Les Jumelles, Les Lan-
gueurs tendres*)
D. Scarlatti—Sonatas for the Harpsichord (Ralph Kirkpatrick) (*Longo*, Nos.
104, 338, 413)
Three-part form:
Haydn—String Quartet, Op. 17, No. V (Minuet)
Ravel—*Le Tombeau de Couperin* (Minuet)
Beethoven—Piano Sonata, Op. 27, No. 1 (Scherzo)
————Piano Sonata, Op. 27, No. 2 (Scherzo)
Chopin—Prelude, Op. 28, No. 15
Rondo:
Haydn—Piano Sonata, No. 9 in D major
Schubert—Piano Sonata, B flat major, Op. Posth. (final movement)
Strauss—*Till Eulenspiegel's Merry Pranks*
Free forms:
Chopin—Prelude, Op. 28, No. 20 (A-B-B)
Schumann—"Frightening" (*Scenes from Childhood*)
(A-B-A-C-A-B-A)

List of Recorded Works

Bartók—Suite, Op. 14 for piano (first and second movements)

List of Recorded Works

Fugue:
Bach—*Well Tempered Clavier*, Books I and II
Concerto grosso:
Bach—*Brandenburg Concerti* Nos. 1–6
Handel—Concerto Grosso, Op. 6, Nos. 1–12
Bloch—Concerto Grosso
Martinu—Concerto Grosso
Chorale prelude:
Bach—Chorale Preludes ("*Orgelbüchlein*")
Motets and madrigals:
Anthologie Sonore—Vol. 2
The Triumphs of Oriana

CHAPTER 13. SONATA FORM

Beethoven—Piano Sonata, Op. 53 ("Waldstein") (see Appendix III)
Symphonies:
Haydn—Symphony No. 102 in B flat major
Mozart—Symphony No. 41 in C major ("Jupiter")
Beethoven—Symphonies Nos. 1–9
Schumann—Symphony No. 4 in D minor (one-movement form)
Mendelssohn—Symphony No. 4 in A major
Brahms—Symphonies Nos. 1–4
Tschaikovsky—Symphony No. 6 in B minor (slow movement at end)
Franck—Symphony in D minor (cyclic form)
Mahler—Symphony No. 2 in C minor (with chorus)
Contemporary symphonies:
Sibelius—Symphony No. 4 in A minor
Prokofieff—Symphony No. 5, Op. 100
Roussel—Symphony No. 3 in G minor
Shostakovitch—Symphony No. 10 in E minor
Honegger—Symphony No. 5
Vaughan Williams—Symphony No. 4 in F minor
Harris—Symphony No. 3 (in one movement)
Piston—Symphony No. 4
Copland—Symphony No. 3
William Schuman—Symphony No. 6 (in one movement)

CHAPTER 14. FREE FORMS

Bach—*Well Tempered Clavier*, Book I, Prelude in B flat major

List of Recorded Works

Bach—Chromatic Fantasy and Fugue in D minor
————Fantasia and Fugue in G minor (organ)
Debussy—*Préludes*, Book II (piano)
Program music:
Jannequin—*Chansons*
Liszt—*Les Préludes*
Saint-Saëns—*Omphale's Spinning Wheel*
Tschaikovsky—*Romeo and Juliet*
Honegger—*Pacific 231*
Ives—*The Unanswered Question*

CHAPTER 15. OPERA AND MUSIC DRAMA

Monteverdi—*Orfeo*
Handel—*Julius Caesar*
Gluck—*Orfeo ed Euridice*
Mozart—*The Magic Flute*
Wagner—*Die Meistersinger*
Verdi—*Otello*
————*Falstaff*
Moussorgsky—*Boris Godounov*
Bizet—*Carmen*
Debussy—*Pelléas et Mélisande*
Berg—*Wozzeck*
Weill—*The Threepenny Opera*
Menotti—*The Consul*
Stravinsky—*The Rake's Progress*

CHAPTER 16. CONTEMPORARY MUSIC

Very easy:
Poulenc—*Le Bal masqué*
Stravinsky—*Petrouchka*
Shostakovitch—Symphony No. 1 in F major, Op. 10
Thomson—*Acadian Songs and Dances* (from *Louisiana Story*)
Quite approachable:
Bloch—*Schelomo*
Villa-Lobos—*Choros* Nos. 4–7
Walton—Concerto for viola
Prokofieff—*Scythian Suite*, Op. 20

List of Recorded Works

Barber—Cello Concerto
Fairly difficult:
Bartók—Sonata for two pianos and percussion
Honegger—Symphony No. 3 (*"Liturgique"*)
Stravinsky—Symphony in C
Piston—Symphony No. 4
Very tough:
Schoenberg—Suite, Op. 29 (Septet)
Webern—Concerto for nine instruments
Varèse—*Ionisation*
Ives—Sonata No. 2 for piano ("Concord, Mass.")
Sessions—String Quartet No. 2
Carter—String Quartet

Suggested Bibliography for Further Reading

HISTORY OF MUSIC

Einstein, Alfred, *A Short History of Music*, New York: Alfred A. Knopf, Inc., 1947.
Nef, Karl, *An Outline of the History of Music*, New York: Columbia University Press, 1935.
Parrish, C., and J. F. Ohl, *Masterpieces of Music before 1750*, New York: W. W. Norton & Company, Inc., 1951.
Sachs, Curt, *Our Musical Heritage: A Short History of Music*, New York: Prentice-Hall, Inc., 1955 (rev. ed.).

MUSICAL ELEMENTS

Erickson, Robert, *The Structure of Music*, New York: Noonday Press, 1955.
Liepmann, Klaus, *The Language of Music*, New York: The Ronald Press Company, 1953.
Newman, William, *Understanding Music*, New York: Harper & Brothers, 1953.

CONTEMPORARY MUSIC

Chase, Gilbert, *America's Music*, New York: McGraw-Hill Book Company, Inc., 1955.

Suggested Bibliography for Further Reading

Copland, Aaron, *Our New Music*, New York: McGraw-Hill Book Company, Inc., 1941.

Lambert, Constant, *Music Ho!* London: Penguin Books, 1948.

Mellers, Wilfrid, *Studies in Contemporary Music*, London: Denis Dobson, Ltd., 1947.

Reis, Claire, *Composers, Conductors, and Critics*, New York: Oxford University Press, 1955.

Stein, Erwin, *Orpheus in New Guises*, London: Rockliff Publishing Corporation, Ltd., 1953.

Ulanov, Barry, *A History of Jazz*, New York: Viking Press, 1952.

THE COMPOSERS SPEAK

Berlioz, Hector, *Memoirs*, New York: Alfred A. Knopf, Inc., 1948.

Copland, Aaron, *Music and Imagination*, Cambridge: Harvard University Press, 1952.

Debussy, Claude A., *Monsieur Croche, the Dilettante Hater*, New York: Lear, 1948.

Hindemith, Paul, *A Composer's World*, Cambridge: Harvard University Press, 1952.

Milhaud, Darius, *Notes without Music*, New York: Alfred A. Knopf, Inc., 1953.

Mozart, W. A., *The Letters of Mozart and His Family* (Emily Anderson, ed. and trans.), New York: The Macmillan Company, 1938. Selections edited by Eric Blom, Penguin edition, 1956.

Nabokov, Nicolas, *Old Friends and New Music*, Boston: Little, Brown & Company, 1951.

Schumann, Robert, *On Music and Musicians*, New York: Pantheon Books, Inc., 1946.

Schoenberg, Arnold, *Style and Idea*, New York: Philosophical Library, Inc., 1950.

Sessions, Roger, *The Musical Experience of Composer, Performer, Listener*, Princeton: Princeton University Press, 1950.

Strauss, Richard, *Recollections and Reflections*, London: Boosey and Hawkes, 1953.

Stravinsky, Igor, *Autobiography*, New York: Simon and Schuster, Inc., 1936.

——*The Poetics of Music*, Cambridge: Harvard University Press, 1947.

Thomson, Virgil, *The Art of Judging Music*, New York: Alfred A. Knopf, Inc., 1948.

Index

[304]

Tone color, mixed, 97
  part played by instruments in,
    80, 84
  single, 87
Tone deafness, 6
Tones, 52–53, 66
Tonic, 53, 70
Toscanini, Arturo, III, 271–273
Traviata (Verdi), 233
Trio for violin, cello, and piano
  (Harris), 58–59
Trio for violin, cello, and piano
  (Ravel), 154
Tristan und Isolde (Wagner), 235
Trombone, 94–95
Trumpet, 94–95
Tschaikovsky, Peter Ilich, 14,
  40–41, 194, 208, 210
Tuba, 95
Twins (Couperin), 130
Two-part (binary form), 120,
  128–131

Varèse, Edgar, 244
Variation, five general types of,
  157
Variation form, 120, 142–159
  basso ostinato, 145–150
  chaconne, 154–156
  passacaglia, 150–154
  theme and variations, 156–159
Variation formulas, examples of
  typical, 276–281
Vaughan Williams, Ralph, 195,
  284

Verdi, Giuseppe, 232–233
Villa-Lobos, Hector, 244
Viola, 88
Violin, 87–88
Violin Sonata (Franck), 163
Vittoria, Tommaso da, 175
Voices in a fugue, 164

Wagner, Richard, 71, 72,
  230–232, 234, 235
"Waldstein" Sonata for piano, Op.
  53 (Beethoven), 191, 286–290
Walküre, Die (Wagner), 231
Walton, William, 195, 244
Weber, Carl Maria von, 59
Webern, Anton, 76, 154, 244
Weill, Kurt, 238
Well Tempered Clavichord (Bach),
  14, 55, 125, 165, 202, 283
Wilbye, John, 175
Wolf, Hugo, 27
Women's Cackle (Jannequin), 208
Woodwind instruments, 87,
  90–93
  bass clarinet, 92–93
  bassoon, 90
  clarinet, 92
  double bassoon, 93
  English horn, 92
  flute, 90–92
  oboe, 91–92
  piccolo, 91
  saxophone, 90–91
Wozzeck (Berg), 154, 236–237